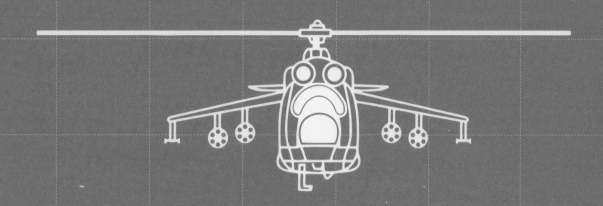

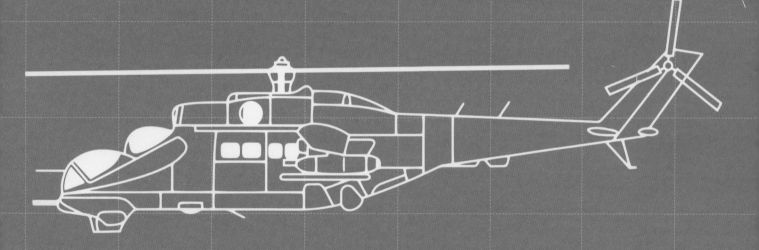

MIL Mi-24 ATTACK HELICOPTER

MIL Mi-24 ATTACK HELICOPTER

In Soviet/Russian and Worldwide Service | 1972 to the Present

MICHAEL NORMANN

4880 Lower Valley Road   Atglen, PA 19310

Originally published as *Mi-24* by Motorbuch Verlag,
Stuttgart © 2016 Motorbuch Verlag
Translated from the German by David Johnston

Library of Congress Control Number: 2019936649

Cover Designed by Justin Watkinson
Type set in Futura Std / Minion Pro

ISBN: 978-0-7643-5867-8
Printed in China

Published by Schiffer Publishing, Ltd.
4880 Lower Valley Road
Atglen, PA 19310
Phone: (610) 593-1777; Fax: (610) 593-2002
E-mail: Info@schifferbooks.com
Web: www.schifferbooks.com

For our complete selection of fine books on this and related
subjects, please visit our website at www.schifferbooks.com.
You may also write for a free catalog.

Schiffer Publishing's titles are available at special discounts
for bulk purchases for sales promotions or premiums. Special
editions, including personalized covers, corporate imprints,
and excerpts, can be created in large quantities for special
needs. For more information, contact the publisher.

We are always looking for people to write books on new and
related subjects. If you have an idea for a book, please contact
us at proposals@schifferbooks.com.

Contents

Venezuelan Mi-35M during a night takeoff. *Sergio J. Padrón A. via Rostvertol PLC*

Foreword

I was eleven when I saw the Mi-24 on television for the first time. An unusually aggressive-looking helicopter rose from behind a woods and hovered briefly in the air. Suddenly a bright spot separated itself and raced away at high speed toward the horizon. A flash of light followed and the turret of a tank that had been hit whirled through the air. That was in the autumn of 1980, when East German television aired a detailed report about the large military exercise Brothers in Arms 80. Flying low to the ground, large numbers of Mi-24s raced over the exercise field. I was impressed.

I fell in love with the Mi-24 from the moment I first saw it, and it was clear to me that I wanted to fly this helicopter when I grew up. Other boys my age dreamed of fast cars or motorcycles. I dreamed of the Mi-24. The goal of being allowed to fly it seemed more realistic to me than to hope to own a fast car in East Germany. I wanted to fly the Mi-24, to tame the power of this highly agile, fierce-looking fighting dragonfly. In the features in the East German media, the Mi-24 pilots swarmed from their machines. When interviewed, one said that flying the Mi-24 was like riding his motorcycle, only better! Because what motorcycle goes 185 miles per hour! I wanted to experience that.

And then a few years later, what has happened to so many before and after me also happened to me. My dream was ruined by a medical examination, with drumbeats and trumpets! Bad luck! A doctor told me that I was not fit to fly, and that was the end of all my dreams. I would never sit in the cockpit of an Mi-24.

They offered me the chance to become an officer, or to work on the Mi-24 as a mechanic. But I didn't want that. Sign up for twenty-five years and then have to watch day after day as others flew the helicopter I had wanted to fly? No, that was not my thing. I took another path. Then came the turning point and everything changed.

More than twenty years later, while conducting research for my book *Helicopters since 1962*, I met a young woman at the booth of the Russian helicopter maker Rostvertol PLC. Her name was Anna Parchomenko. We began a conversation. I dug out my schoolbook Russian, which I had not needed for almost a quarter of a century and was therefore badly atrophied. She tried a few words of German. Anna listened to my request for photos and information, and at some point, after I told her that flying the Mi-24 had once been my dream, she asked me why I didn't write a book about the helicopter. A few years later I decided to turn this suggestion into action. Than you, Anna—that was a very good idea. And as I am thanking people, I would also like to say a big thank-you to the enthusiasts of the Cottbus Airfield Museum. They obligingly opened the doors of their Mi-24D and allowed me to sit in the cockpit—a great experience! For me it was close to the fulfillment of a childhood dream. And so I made it into the cockpit of an Mi-24 after all!

I would also like to thank all those who helped me in the creation of this book with their assistance and advice, with pictures and ideas. Without their help this book would not have turned out as well as it did.

And now it is time for us to climb into the Mi-24. Despite all the fascination, which I understand very well and also share, I would like readers to remember one thing: the Mi-24 is a weapon. And the best thing one can say about a weapon is "I never had to use it in anger." Unfortunately this is not true of the Mi-24. It has often had to show in anger what it can do. It often had to bite, and it did so very well. Not for nothing was and is it affectionately called "the Crocodile" by its pilots. To many it remains the best attack helicopter in the world.

Michael Normann
Rödgen, Germany, 2016

The Path to
the Attack Helicopter

The Mi-24 was the Soviet Union's first true attack helicopter. It was built in large numbers and exported to many nations in the world. The Mi-24 served as the standard attack helicopter of the Warsaw Pact, the Eastern defense alliance, and became famous as the most dangerous and effective weapon used by the Soviets in Afghanistan. The Mi-24 serves in many military forces around the world, and in many places it still proves itself day after day in training and combat.

The Mi-24 is a representative of a unique helicopter concept. It is the only attack helicopter in the world that was developed in keeping with the concept of the "flying armored personnel carrier." The only truly comparable helicopter was the elegant Sikorsky S-67, which unfortunately never made the jump to operational service.

The Mi-24 is synonymous with the design of Soviet/Russian attack helicopters in general. This book is dedicated to it.

The Concept of the Flying Armored Personnel Carrier

The Mi-24 did not come from nothing. Its creation was heavily influenced by the development of attack helicopters in the Western world, specifically the United States. It was the response to efforts being made there to create a new class of weapon.

I have allowed myself a brief digression at the beginning of this book, which is intended to describe the path that led to the creation of a Soviet attack helicopter.

The Soviet approach to the creation of an attack helicopter differed from that of the Americans, in that it was a "scientifically based process." This was in contrast to the trial-and-error method, cautiously approaching the solution to a problem, as practiced by the US. The Soviet developers selected a path that seemed dictated to them by the prevailing philosophy in the USSR at that time.

A tenet of that philosophy said that "everything and everyone in nature and society is in a constant state of change and development" and that development would always take place from simple (lower) to complex (higher). This higher development could take place in linear form or in waves. At the end of a development stage, so they believed, would stand a revolutionary breakthrough that would lead to a new, more highly advanced level of development.

So much for that theory, which appealed to Soviet military scientists, who postulated that such trends could also be observed in the development of military technology. Not entirely wrongly, they pointed to the continuing tendency toward ever more complex, more capable, and of course more expensive weapons systems.

From this realization came the thesis that one could estimate the future direction of the development of military technology, if one could determine the premises on which the development of every technology was based. And the Soviet military scientists believed that they had found one such development criterion. It was the mobility-of-troops factor.

The starting point for consideration was the common soldier. Whether an ancient Greek hoplite, Landsknecht mercenary, or modern infantryman, the soldier's mobility was very limited. On average he moved forward at about 3 miles an hour and could cover 15 to 18 miles per day. Of course, more-rapid movement was possible for brief periods, but as seen over the long run, this figure remained. More distance was not feasible over longer periods without reducing the soldier's fighting abilities.

The use of the horse represented the first revolutionary leap toward increased mobility. With the aid of the horse, whether as a draft, pack, or riding animal, the mobility of the soldier rose considerably. Freed from the burden of a heavy pack, the soldier could march for greater distances, and, mounted, he could cover much-greater distances per day. With the use of the horse came the first trend toward specialization. On the one hand the horse was used purely as a means of transportation, while on the other hand, in the other specialization direction, the horse was used as a weapon.

The battle horse was born. At times these animals were even protected by armor.

The second revolutionary leap to improve the mobility of soldiers was introduced by the trail-breaking development of the internal-combustion engine. Automobiles and trucks were created in rapid succession. With the help of these vehicles, soldiers could now be transported over great distances at speeds that must have seemed unimaginable at the time. These vehicles were ill suited for use in combat, however, since they offered the soldiers being transported no protection of any kind against enemy rifle fire and shell fragments. The result was the armored automobile, which first appeared before the start of the First World War. In this development the Soviet scientists believed they had found a new law, which was that for every mode of transportation there would have to be an armored, combat-capable counterpart. The horse became the armored battle horse, and the truck became the armored automobile.

Since the armored automobile did not exactly prove itself in the First World War, this subsequently led to a revolutionary further development. The simple transport truck became an armored troop transport (бронетранспортер), and the battle tank (танк) took the place of the armored automobile.

The combination of battle tank and armored personnel carrier was employed decisively during the Second World War. The dualism of means of transportation and combat vehicle remained.

This was also true of developments in the 1950s and 1960s. Here the Soviet military scientists saw the trend toward the creation of a standard tank. This was supposed to dispense with the plethora of tank types used to date, and to contribute to simplified logistics. The standard tank was supposed to combine the speed of a light tank with the firepower and armor protection of a heavy tank, and all this, if possible, in the medium weight class.

Significant improvements in the means of transporting infantry could also be seen in the future, or so they believed. In order not only to accompany the tank on the battlefield, but also to be able to work effectively with it, the infantryman of the future would go into battle in armored fighting vehicles. These machines would not just be armored transporters but would also have to be capable of successfully engaging any enemy, including tanks. Such a vehicle they designated BMP, or *boyevaya mashina pekhoty* (боевая машина пехота), which translated into

English means "infantry fighting machine." The term "infantry fighting vehicle," or IFV, became embedded in American parlance.

With their heavy armaments, armored personnel carriers were supposed to be capable of destroying any type of tank then in use, at the same time offering protection for its crew and the infantry it was carrying against fragments and light weapons, and of course being able to cover great distances at high speed.

Soviet military scientists believed that the standard tank and the armored personnel carriers represented the provisional high point in the development of ground-based means to improve the soldier's mobility.

The next revolutionary step in the improvement of the soldier's mobility was made possible by the invention of the helicopter. With its help, it was now possible to move troops quickly over great

Mikhail Leontyevich Mil.
Rostvertol PLC Archive

distances, regardless of terrain, and deliver them to places that previously would have been difficult to access.

The developments on the American side were watched by the Soviets, and the formation there of air cavalry units seemed to confirm the predicted revolutionary advance in the mobility of the soldier.

In the Soviet Union, it was believed that the future development of the helicopter would roughly follow the previous development of land-based modes of transportation. Transport helicopters would be joined by attack helicopters. In a later stage the transport helicopter would be armed and armored, and the attack helicopter could represent a modern equivalent of the standard battle tank. One of the main proponents of this theme was the gifted Soviet helicopter designer Mikhail Leontyevich Mil.

While observing American activities during the early stages of the Vietnam War, Soviet military experts concluded that the helicopters in use at that time were still at the level of unarmored transport machines. The AH-1G Cobra attack helicopters sent to Vietnam to support them were seen as a simple interim solution on the same level as the armored automobile or the simple tank.

The helicopter created by the Advanced Aerial Fire Support System (AAFSS) competition in the US was regarded by the Soviets as a true attack helicopter.

AH-G Cobra in a firefight during the Vietnam War. *US DoD*

AH-56 Cheyenne. *Lockheed*

Objekt 764

Object 764 was the forerunner of the modern armored personnel carrier.

It combined light armor with what was for its time outstanding firepower. A coaxial machine gun was provided to engage soft targets, while the long-range *Malyutka* antitank missile was capable of destroying enemy tanks beyond effective cannon fire range. At shorter ranges it could employ its 73 mm Grom smooth-bore gun. Its hollow-charge shells could easily penetrate the armor of all battle tanks then known to be in service.

It was thus a logical and obvious step for Mikhail Leontyevich Mil, who was enthused by the BMP concept, to develop an attack helicopter that would combine armor against small-arms fire with a capable, tank-destroying armament and also be capable of transporting the same number of soldiers as a BMP-1.

As soon as this flying armored personnel carrier became operational, they could begin development of a highly modern flying standard battle tank. At least that was the plan.

Mikhail Mil had presented the idea of an attack helicopter to head of state Nikita Khruschev and his entourage in 1963. While defense minister Malinovsky was vehemently opposed to attack helicopters, his deputy Grechko was immediately enthused by Mil's proposal. Khruschev put a quick end to the ensuing discussion between the high-ranking military men by ordering them to "kindly shut their traps." Khruschev thought just as little of the idea of an attack helicopter as he did of heavy tanks and aircraft carriers.

The AH-56 Cheyenne was regarded as the main competition. A future Soviet attack helicopter would have to be capable of standing up against the Cheyenne.

They were, however, conscious that the development of such a flying standard tank would be a lengthy and expensive process. Development delays had to be expected. In order to provide their own military with an attack helicopter in the foreseeable future, one or more interim steps would have to be taken. The result was an armed and armored transport helicopter equivalent to the armored personnel carrier (Mi-8TB); however, it would scarcely be capable of defending against large-scale attacks by enemy tanks.

The opportunity to solve this problem presented itself in the form of the armored personnel carrier concept developed at the Chelyabinsk Tractor Works. Developed there in 1964–65 was the Object 764, which was the direct predecessor of the later BMP-1.

The BMP-1 served as Mikhail L. Mil's model for the development of a future attack helicopter. *Konflikty.pl*

Two years later, Mil had the opportunity to visit the Paris Air Salon at Le Bourget. There he saw his estimation that the Soviet Union was three to four years ahead of the West in the field of civilian helicopters confirmed. In the field of military helicopters, however, they were hopelessly behind. While Western manufacturers were already offering guided antitank missiles as an optional armament for helicopters, because of Khruschev's aversion to armed helicopters, in the Soviet Union they were standing still. Not until Khruschev was forced to step down in 1966 would the picture change. Mil's idea of creating a battle helicopter would get its chance.

Project V-24

The creation of air-mobile infantry units by the US Army (Air Cavalry) was watched carefully by the Soviet military. Naturally there was a growing desire to do the same as the competition and form similar units themselves.

The simplest approach to forming their own air assault units was to copy the American concept of air cavalry. This was not possible, however, since there was

no helicopter in the Soviet arsenal in the performance class of the American workhorse, the UH-1 Huey.

The nearest Soviet equivalent to the UH-1 was the Mi-2, code-named Hoplite by NATO, but it was regarded as too small, with an inadequate performance. The Mi-2 could never accommodate eight to ten soldiers. The nearest alternative was the Mi-8, which was a class larger than the UH-1 and could transport not only an infantry squad, but also an entire platoon. The huge Mi-6 helicopter, which was also available, could even transport an entire company, and the W-12, which was under development, could accommodate an entire battalion. However, there was no helicopter in the size class of the UH-1.

The OKB Mil therefore began work on the V-22 project. In principle it was a clone of the Mi-2 and UH-1. As the Mi-22, this helicopter was supposed to carry out the same roles in future Soviet air assault units as the UH-1 had in the US Air Cavalry.

As the leading advocate of the "flying armored personnel carrier" concept, however, Mikhail Mil was not really convinced by the V-22. Lessons from the Vietnam War showed that such light, unarmored helicopters could be used successfully only if the enemy had no organized air defense. As soon as the

The AH-G Cobra regularly flew escort for American transport helicopters. *US Army*

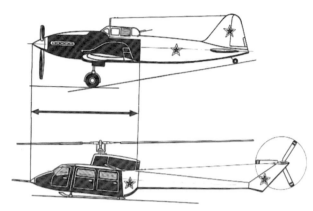

Comparison of the armor protection of the V-24 with that of the Il-2. *OKB Mil*

Mockup of the V-24. *OKB Mil*

Like the BMP-1, the attack helicopter was also supposed to accommodate eight soldiers. *OKB Mil*

enemy was in a position to field even the simplest antiaircraft weapons, the crews and troops in the unarmored transport helicopters would be in danger. Even concentrated fire from assault rifles such as the legendary AK-47 Kalashnikov would be capable of inflicting heavy losses on unarmored helicopters. Support from escorting attack helicopters such as the AH-1 Cobra helped reduce losses, but they remained unusually high. More than 6,000 American helicopters were lost during the Vietnam War.

Mil asked himself why he should copy such an unprotected transport system, and whether it would not be better to derive a flying armored personnel carrier from the V-22 concept. Thus was born the idea for the V-24 project.

Mil designed a version of the V-22, added stub wings and 0.3 inches of armor, hung pylons for antitank missiles beneath the wings, and mounted a 23 mm twin-barreled cannon to the helicopter's starboard skid. A mockup of the helicopter was built and shown to high-ranking members of the military.

The V-24 model held two pilots and eight soldiers, demonstrating the helicopter's transport capacity. The powerful armament suggested that the combat dragonfly would be able to shoot its own way out of traps and would be thoroughly capable of providing effective fire support to soldiers dropped off in a contested landing zone. Questions about its relatively thin armor were answered by pointing out that the Ilyushin Il-2 *Sturmovik*, the legendary close-support aircraft of the Great Patriotic War, had been no better armored, and that this armor had proved completely adequate.

The reaction of the military was twofold. Young military theoreticians and representatives of the air force and army military academies were more than impressed by the V-24 project. The military bureaucrats of the defense ministry under Marshall Malinovsky, however, had other, rather conservative views as to how to equip future units of the Soviet army—namely, with standard battle tanks, long-range artillery, and fighter-bombers with variable-geometry wings.

Despite everything, Mil succeeded in selling the concept of the flying armored personnel carrier well enough to be awarded a development contract. An invitation to tender was issued, and the Soviet Union's two helicopter design bureaus were each issued orders to create a project for an attack helicopter with added troop-carrying capacity.

While the design by the OKB Kamov was rather uninspiring (they simply took the existing Ka-25 naval helicopter, modified the nose a little, replaced the wheeled undercarriage with skids, and stuck a machine gun turret under the nose), the OKB Mil in Moscow set to work seriously and with great enthusiasm.

The OKB Mil worked out several variants of a future attack helicopter that differed in size and power plants. In addition to a single-engine variant weighing about 7.7 tons, which was largely based on the still-uncompleted V-22, consideration was given to developing a twin-engine attack helicopter in the 11-ton class. The twin-engine helicopter was to follow the existing and proven concept of the OKB Mil's turbine-powered helicopters. This meant that it would be a helicopter with a conventional layout with main and tail rotors. Its two engines would be placed close together and in front of the main rotor transmission. The selected power plants were the TV3-117 turbine engines in development for the Mi-14, which promised to be the equal of any Western engine of similar size.

Skids were done away with in favor of a proven retractable tricycle undercarriage.

Since the design bureau had achieved good results with stub wings on the giant Mi-6 helicopter, it planned to equip the attack helicopter with them as well. The designers hoped that the use of stub wings would allow them to kill two birds with one stone. On the one hand, during forward flight the stub wings would produce a considerable amount of lift and thus unload the main rotor, and on the other hand, pylons could be slung beneath the stub wings for the carriage of bombs, unguided rockets, or fuel tanks.

It was envisaged that in addition to the systems mentioned above, the armament of the V-24, which internally was called the Mi-24 from the beginning, would include Falanga antitank missiles and a GSh-23 cannon in a revolving turret.

This drawing illustrates a variant of the V-24 investigated by Mil. *OKB Mil*

The guided antitank missiles would be mounted in pairs on each side of the helicopter's fuselage. For the cannon they borrowed an idea from the Americans. It was planned, like on the AH-56 Cheyenne, to enable the gunner's seat to pivot, so that he would always be looking in the direction in which the gun was pointing.

To ensure that the gunner had a view to all sides, the cockpit had to be designed with a tandem layout. The gunner was placed in front, with the pilot seated behind him.

For a long time in the OKB Mil there had been disagreement as to the layout of the V-24, and so three different mockups of the complete helicopter and five different variants of the fuselage nose were built. A common feature of all these variants was that their propulsion and rotor systems were based on the tried-and-true dynamic systems of the Mi-8.

Among the variants there were more or less elegant layouts; the mounting of the antitank missiles varied between simple racks and small wings in canard configuration. The stub wings were either smaller versions of the Mi-6 wings or wings with a slight amount of anhedral.

The mockups were shown to the military, which selected one of the externally unattractive layout variants. They also requested changes. Representatives of the defense ministry thought that the use of a 23 mm cannon was excessive. They favored following the example of the Americans, who used rotary machine guns on their helicopters in Vietnam, and demanded the use of a similar weapons system, but with a caliber of 12.7 mm. The Falanga antitank missile was also rejected. Its place was to be taken by the Shturm system, which had yet to be developed.

Objections that the requested changes might delay development of the helicopter were simply brushed aside by the representatives of the military bureaucracy.

On May 6, 1968, the OKB Mil officially received the contract to begin development of an attack helicopter.

As general designer, Mikhail Mil exercised overall control of Project V-24, and after his death in 1970, his place was taken by Marat Tishchenko. Direct development work was managed by deputy chief designer V. Kuznetsov, one of the most experienced designers of helicopters in the Soviet Union. V. Olshevets worked on the V-24 as chief designer, and S. Sernov and V. Smuislov were responsible for flight testing.

The requirements placed on the new machine were high. It was to have a maximum speed that could not be less than 200 to 217 mph. Static ceiling had to be in the area of 4,900 to 6,560 feet, even in high temperatures, and maximum payload could not be less than 1.9 tons. The customer also demanded that the Mi-24 possess outstanding maneuverability and have sufficient power reserves to enable it to engage enemy helicopters in air-to-air combat. It had to be capable of using its armament accurately from a hover and in flight.

The customer also demanded that the Mi-24 be able to carry external loads and achieve speeds of between 62 and 155 miles per hour (mph).

Work on the project proceeded rapidly at Mil. In August 1968, workers began cutting metal for the first prototypes. By February 1969, work was so far advanced that the mockup of the future attack helicopter could be shown to a state and party delegation. And during the course of the same year, Mil was able to complete the first prototype. The unusually high pace of completion of the project was due to the fact that in developing the Mi-24, Mil had tried to use tried elements of the Mi-8 and Mi-14 helicopters wherever possible. Essentially this affected the power plants, the transmission, the power transfer mechanisms, and the main and tail rotors. In this way, development risks could be minimized and the pace increased.

The Isotov TV3-117 was selected to power the helicopter. This engine had been derived from the TV2-117 of the Mi-8 and delivered the desired increase in performance. It was not self-starting, however, and starting the engine therefore required a small AI-9V auxiliary turbine.

The TV3-117 had a standard output of 1,700 hp. In an emergency, such as the loss of an engine, the remaining engine could produce an emergency output of 2,200 hp for a short time.

Integration of the TV3-117 into the overall Mi-24 system proved somewhat tricky at first, as Mi-24 test pilot German Alfyorov recalled while reminiscing in a Russian television documentary about the Mi-24. The prototype engines initially installed had an operating life of just two (!) hours. They proved to be temperamental, and the test pilots had to expect something unusual to happen during every flight. Sometimes the engine reacted very slowly to power reductions, but the next time they simply flooded when handled the same way. There were engine stalls and other unpleasant occurrences. The technicians had their hands full. But when after some time the problems were finally managed, it turned out that the TV3-117 was one of the best helicopter engines in the world.

While the helicopter itself and its power plants could be developed quite quickly and work therefore progressed rapidly, development of the electronic and optical elements, plus the weapons system, proved complicated. This was in part due to meddling "from above."

In the mentioned television documentary, former Mil chief designer Yevgeni Yablonski described a conference held by Dementyev, the minister for aircraft construction, at which representatives of the OKB Mil were supposed to report on the Mi-24 project's state of progress. After speaking for about ten minutes, the OKB representative was abruptly interrupted by the minister and asked why they were trying to reinvent the wheel. There were already comparable sensor, navigation, and weapons systems in the union, and these should be integrated into the Mi-24. It was not necessary to invent a new navigation system if the Puma system developed for the Su-24 was modified and used in the Mi-24. A special targeting system for the helicopter's cannon was unnecessary, since there was already the KPS-53 system in the Tu-22, which must be applied to the Mi-24. A new revolving turret for the weapon was also unnecessary; it could be taken from other bombers. And there was much more.

The decision was nonsense, but in the Soviet Union orders were orders. And an order had to be followed, cost what it may. And so the Mil collective was forced to get by with components that were neither tailored to a helicopter nor harmonized with each other. Matters were made worse by the fact that the manufacturers and developers of the components required by ministerial order showed no interest in modifying them for the Mi-24. The mass ideology prevailed in Soviet industry. Makers of components were looked upon with favor if they produced in large numbers. Variants of products, which of course

Artist's conception of the V-22. Its service designation would have been Mi-22. *OKB Mil*

lowered the total production number, were therefore avoided and rejected by the manufacturers. The conflict between innovative-development bureaus and conservative manufacturers was more or less preordained. A clear system of leadership, which could have overcome this problem, was almost completely lacking.

The OKB Mil therefore had to make great efforts to somehow make the incompatible components compatible. This of course cost valuable time.

Looking back, it can be said that the ministerial decision delayed development of the Mi-24 attack helicopter by several years.

* The word Union (*Soyuz*) was often used in the Soviet Union when speaking about the entire nation. *Sovyetsky Soyuz* was too long for normal usage; therefore *Soyuz* was often used when referring to the USSR.

Mi-24 Versions

Brief Overview

In its initial stages, development of the Mi-24 attack helicopter was hampered by a number of serious delays. In particular, it was problems in development of the weapons system that caused delays and forced the OKB Mil to adopt interim solutions just to get the Mi-24 into production. In the course of time, the planned sequence of operational versions that were supposed to be developed deviated considerably from the sequence that was actually achieved.

The OKB originally envisaged equipping the first production version of the Mi-24 with a 12.7 mm Yak-B rotary machine gun, which was to be housed in a remotely controlled chin turret, and with the Falanga-P guided antitank missile, which was a very advanced weapon at that time. This version was supposed to receive the internal designation *isdeliye* 241 (Product 241).

The designation Product 242 (*isdeliye* 242) was envisaged for a developed version with the newly developed Shturm guided antitank missile demanded by the military. It was expected that it would be followed by a variant with a heavier cannon armament (*isdeliye* 243). A pilot-training variant was supposed to close out the Mi-24 family of versions. This version was taken into the plan as *isdeliye* 244.

Further Mi-24 versions were not planned, since the follow-up V-28 model was already in the starting blocks.

But the reality looked much different. Since neither the Yak-B nor the Shturm were available, the OKB Mil turned to existing, less capable weapons systems for the Mi-24. The result was the stopgap solution *isdeliye* 245, which entered service as the Mi-24A. When the Yak-B became available some time later, *isdeliye* 241 was realized as the Mi-24B.

Quantity production did not begin, however, because in the meantime it was possible to conclude work on a new fuselage nose. Because the Shturm guided antitank missile was still not available, the Mi-24B's weapons system was incorporated into *isdeliye* 246, which rolled off the production lines in large numbers as the Mi-24D.

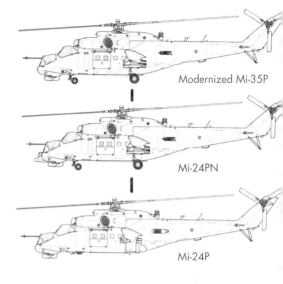

Modernized Mi-35P

Mi-24PN

Mi-24P

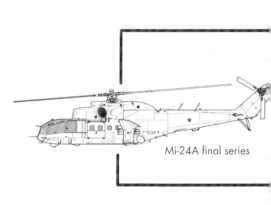

Mi-24A final series

The sequence of Mi-24 variant designations was supposed to be alphabetic. Therefore the gap between the Mi-24B and Mi-24D jumped out immediately. In the Cyrillic alphabet his gap covered two letters, V and G, rather than the one letter in our alphabet.

The V had already been issued for *isdeliye* 242, the first Mi-24 variant with the Shturm guided antitank missile. Logically, therefore, the interim model should have been called Mi-24G.

The OKB quite intentionally avoided using the G, however, because they wanted to prevent the interim variant from being given the offensive nickname

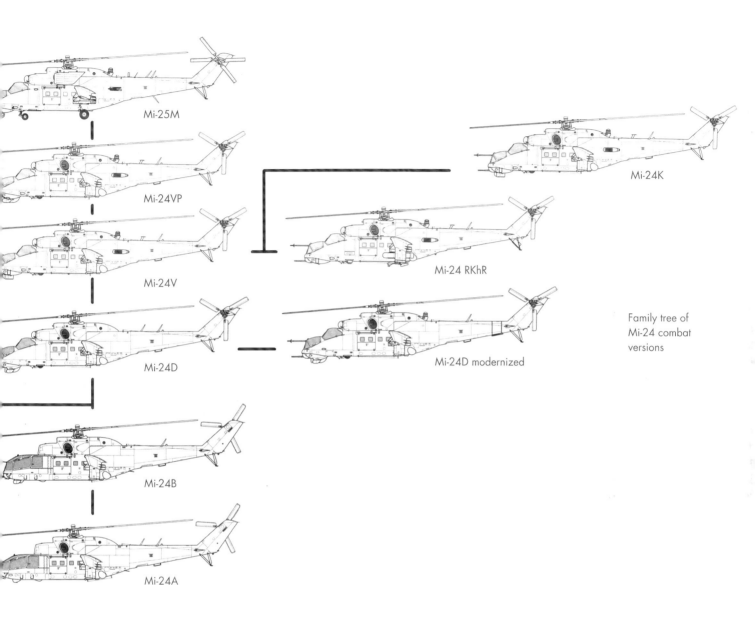

Mi-25M

Mi-24VP

Mi-24V

Mi-24D

Mi-24B

Mi-24A

Mi-24K

Mi-24 RKhR

Mi-24D modernized

Family tree of
Mi-24 combat
versions

Govno, which is an expletive whose closest equivalent in English is "shit." It is bleeped out on television, and the French elegantly rewrite it as *merde*! For aesthetic reasons, therefore, the Mi-24G unceremoniously became the Mi-24D. After the Mi-24D entered production, a training helicopter was derived from it and given the name Mi-24DU (*isdeliye* 249).

When the Shturm finally became available, *isdeliye* 242 became a reality and entered service as the Mi-24V.

A few years later, the previous tradition of arranging versions alphabetically was broken. Therefore *isdeliye*

243 was given the index *P*. The letter *P* stood for *pushka* (cannon) or *pushetshny* (cannon armed).

From the Mi-24V were derived special versions for reconnaissance, fire control, and the chemical service; before at the end of the 1980s, the Mi-24VP was created.

For export there were simplified versions designated Mi-25 and Mi-35. Further development of the Mi-24 continued after the fall of the Soviet Union.

What follows are descriptions of the individual Mi-24 versions.

Mi-24 Prototype (*isdeliye 240*)

The twin-engined V-24 attack helicopter had a classic rotor system with a five-blade main rotor and a three-blade tail rotor. The main rotor was tilted 2.3 degrees to the right of the helicopter's longitudinal axis. This was supposed to ensure stable flight and improve the accuracy of the aircraft's machine guns and unguided rockets.

Depending on airspeed, the stub wings produced 19 to 25 percent of the lift and thus prevented loading of the main rotor. They were not only designed as lift-producing units but were also envisaged for transport of part of the armament.

The helicopter airframe had an aerodynamically favorable, streamlined, slim shape in order to minimize drag.

The crew cabin was laid out as a tandem cockpit. The gunner sat forward; the pilot, offset slightly to the left, sat behind him. In the OKB Mil, the crew cabin was more or less jokingly called the "veranda," in part because the large glazed areas were reminiscent of a veranda, and in part because the sun's rays could create high temperatures like a greenhouse in the cockpit. The front of the crew cabin was protected by a thick armor glass panel. Nevertheless, from the beginning a sort of head armor was considered necessary for the crew. Protective vests came years later, during the war in Afghanistan.

The role of the V-24's gunner was to search for targets, then locate and identify them. To engage them he could choose to use the aircraft's flexibly mounted machine gun, drop bombs, or use guided antitank missiles. The gunner's position in the prototypes was not equipped with all the control instruments that would have enabled him to fly the helicopter in an emergency.

The pilot in the rear seat controlled the flight of the helicopter. He could attack targets with unguided rockets. If required, he could also fire the helicopter's machine gun; however, it was necessary to lock the weapon in its neutral position.

Up to eight troops could be carried in the V-24's cargo compartment. There were two rows of benches for them, fixed in the center of the area. The soldiers sat back to back. Four soldiers faced to port, the other four to starboard. They were able to enter or leave the helicopter quickly through large folding doors on both sides of the fuselage, which opened upward and downward. The bottom halves of the doors were equipped with footholds for easy entry. The freight area's ceiling was low, making it impossible for the men to stand upright.

The first Mi-24 prototypes were equipped with stub wings that resembled those used by the Mi-6 giant helicopter. *OKB Mil*

To protect the soldiers, the doors were armored against small-arms fire. The windows opened, allowing the troops to fire their personal weapons. There was a bracket for an assault rifle or machine gun in each window. For weapons of the AK-47 family there were bore evacuators, which could be attached to the Kalashnikov's case cover and vent the powder gases outside via a flexible hose.

The cockpit and cargo area were designed so that they could be hermetically sealed in an emergency. With the windows closed, a certain overpressure was created in the area, which was supposed to prevent radioactive dust and poisonous gases from entering. The required compressed air was bled from the engine's seventh compressor stage and fed into the cabin via a filter.

As previously mentioned, eight fully equipped soldiers could be carried in the freight cabin. It was also possible to carry four prone casualties or up to 4,400 pounds of freight.

On the outside of the fuselage, racks were attached on each side for carriage of two Falanga-M guided antitank missiles. They were, however, so unfortunately placed that they significantly hampered rapid entry or egress by the soldiers.

Elements of the electronic and radio equipment were housed in the aft fuselage and tail boom.

The V-24 was equipped with the VUAP-1 (ВУАП-1) autopilot, as well as the SAU-V24 (САУ-В24) navigation system. Navigation equipment also included the DISS-15 (ДИСС-15) Doppler navigation system, which with the help of a radar altimeter and by considering the Doppler effect could determine the helicopter's position and display it on a map in the cockpit.

The tail fin was relatively large, with an asymmetric profile to unload the tail rotor at high speeds. At maximum flying speed, the tail fin, with an area of 10.75 square meters, generated two-thirds of the necessary force needed for torque balance.

The V-24 was the first Soviet helicopter with a retractable undercarriage. The nosewheel retracted rearward. It did not retract completely, so that it could act as a shock absorber in the event of a crash landing. The wheels of the main undercarriage were retracted into the fuselage and, when retracted, were completely covered by oversized undercarriage doors.

The V-24's fuel capacity was 561 US gallons; the fuel was carried in five self-sealing tanks. For increased range it was possible to carry additional fuel in two auxiliary tanks in the freight compartment. These increased fuel capacity by a further 430 gallons.

An early Mi-24 prototype during a test flight. *Russkiye Vertolyoty*

The V-24's hydraulic system was designed to be triple redundant to improve the helicopter's survivability under fire.

Since the planned Shturm and Yak-B weapons systems were not yet available, the V-24 prototypes were equipped with the K4V weapons complex (К4В), which had already proved itself on the armed variants of the Mi-4 and Mi-8. It included the 9M17 Falanga-M guided antitank missile (ракет 9М17 комплекса "Фаланга-М") system, in which the missiles had to be steered manually by the gunner. He was provided with a 9Sha121 sight (9Ш121), whose optics provided up to 8x magnification. The control signals were transmitted to the rocket by radio.

An Afanasyev A 12.7 mm machine gun was mounted in the NUV-1 (НУВ-1) weapons station in the nose.

Each of the weapons pylons under the stub wings could carry a UB-32 rocket pod for S-5 unguided rockets. Alternative loads included 100 kg (220 lb.) and 250 kg (550 lb.) bombs. One 500 kg (1,100 lb.) bomb or a napalm canister could be mounted on each stores rack.

An OPB-1R (ОПБ-1Р) bombsight was present in the cockpit for use with unguided bombs. The Mi-24's pilot was responsible for the use of unguided rockets. He used a simple PKV sight (ПКВ) as a targeting aid.

Factory testing of the V-24 began on September 15, 1969. The first few times the helicopter lifted off, it was tethered by cables to the ground. After completion of the tethered flights, on the fourth day of trials the first free flight was made. At the controls of the V-24 was test pilot German Alfyorov.

Two prototypes were built at the Moscow helicopter factory for flight testing. They were followed by ten preproduction aircraft, of which five were built in Moscow and the rest at Helicopter Factory No. 116 in the West Siberian city of Arsenyev, where mass production was to take place. Several of the prototypes built at Arsenyev remained there, and the rest were sent to the flight-testing center in Moscow for flight trials. They were initially used for flight and weapons trials, but later they were used to test various modifications and as the starting point for new versions of the helicopter.

Factory testing was followed by state trials, which began in June 1970 and lasted half a year. These flight trials were very intensive. In the overwhelming majority of trials, the values achieved by the prototypes confirmed the estimated performance figures.

There were also problems, however. At first the service life of several components was unsatisfactory. The same was true of the structural strength of some assemblies. These problems were solved through reworking, such as replacing steel with titanium in some highly loaded assemblies. The cause of excessive vibration in several flight regimes was also found. The V-24's fuselage vibrations were subsequently found to be relatively minor compared to those of the Mi-8, despite the former's significantly greater speed.

There were also difficulties that were not solved so easily and quickly, however. Among them was a phenomenon that in Russian is called *gollandski shag* (голландский шаг), or Dutch roll in English. It is a combination of yawing and rolling oscillations that lead to an uncomfortable flight condition, which to an observer outside the aircraft gives the impression of it being flown by a drunk person. To maintain a stable attitude, the pilot is forced to constantly compensate and take countermeasures. The V-24 began encountering the Dutch roll problem at speeds in excess of 120 mph if the helicopter was being flown without assistance from the autopilot.

To counter these stability problems, the designers decided to redesign the V-24's stub wings. The straight wings of the type used by the Mi-6 were replaced with wings with 12 degrees of anhedral. The new stub wings were also fitted with two pylons each for the carriage of bombs and rocket pods. During weapons trials, fears arose that firing unguided rockets during aggressive maneuvering might result in the rockets striking the guided antitank missiles mounted on the pylons on the forward fuselage. It was also suspected that the guided antitank missiles might possibly strike the helicopter's fuselage after takeoff. The launch rails were therefore moved from fuselage-mounted pylons to the wingtips. Pylons were mounted on the wingtips, on which the launch rails for the guided antitank missiles were attached. Thus the V-24 received its characteristic frontal silhouette.

During trials it was discovered that the components of the Raduga-F targeting system associated with the Falanga guided antitank missile complex were too large to fit inside the V-24's cockpit. The Yak-B machine gun, which was still in testing, and especially the remotely controlled USPU-24 turret, also proved much larger than anticipated. The Mil designers were therefore forced to lengthen the cabins of the prototypes. During the redesigning of the cockpit, the gunner's position was provided with a joystick, collective lever, and pedals to enable the gunner to fly the aircraft if the pilot was disabled.

The modification work was carried out parallel to the mounting of the newly developed wings and completed at the end of 1970. The same modifications were carried out on several prototypes and all preproduction aircraft.

Because the Yak-B and the Shturm guided antitank missile were still not available at that time, the state flight trials were carried out and passed with the available weapons systems.

In 1971, the V-24 officially entered service with the Soviet military. Henceforth it was designated the Mi-24A (Ми-24А). The internal company designation was *isdeliye* 245 (Изделие 245).

Mi-24A (*isdeliye* 245)

Even before the completion of state flight trials, at the end of 1970, the new helicopter was placed in production at Factory 116 in Arsenyev, and deliveries to the armed forces began in 1971. By the time production ceased in 1974, approximately 240 aircraft had left the production line.

The design bureau, along with the manufacturer and the military, regarded the Mi-24A (Ми-24А, Изделие 245) strictly as an interim type. It was initially planned that the prototypes would be followed by a production model equipped with the Falanga guided antitank missile and the rapid-firing Yak-B 12.7 (*isdeliye* 241). It was to be followed by a new version with the Shturm guided antitank missile (*isdeliye* 242) and then by a planned version with heavier cannon armament (*isdeliye* 243). The *isdeliye* 244 was supposed to be a pure training version of the Mi-24.

Even before flight testing was completed, it was obvious that the Yak-B would not be ready in time, and it was decided to produce an interim variant of the Mi-24. Following the logical sequence of designations, this interim solution was given the product number *isdeliye* 245.

The first examples of the Mi-24A to be completed were delivered to the Soviet military's helicopter training center near the city of Voronezh. The first frontline unit to receive the Mi-24 was stationed in the Far East near Vladivostok, a location that by Soviet standards was very close to the factory in Arsenyev that produced the helicopter.

The selection of this location followed a Soviet tradition, in which units based near the producing factory were the first to receive new military technology. This had the advantage that in case serious technical problems should appear that could not be dealt with by military service personnel during the technology's introduction phase, specialists from the manufacturer could be on the scene quickly.

The pilots of active helicopter units regarded the Mi-24A with mixed feelings. On the one hand, they were enthusiastic about the breathtaking performance and the outstanding handling of the new attack helicopter. The Mi-24A was clearly faster and much more agile than the Mi-4M and Mi-8TB helicopters they had flown to date. For many pilots, therefore, flying the Mi-24 was a dream; however, they were less than enthusiastic about its weapons system. In principle it was the same as that of the Mi-4M, and compared to the Mi-8B it was even seen as a step backward. The Mi-8TB could carry six rocket pods and six Malyutka guided antitank missiles. The Mi-24A, on the other hand, could carry only four UB-32 rocket pods and an equal number of Falanga-M guided antitank missiles.

An Mi-24 prototype with planned weapons array was displayed during a presentation for the party and state leadership of the USSR. *OKB Mil*

While the range of the Falanga-M was superior to that of the Malyutka, the system's accuracy was relatively poor and was dependent on the abilities of the gunner. On average, just three out of ten missiles found their targets.

The A-12.7 machine gun used by the Mi-24A was considered a reliable weapon, but its rate of fire was much too low. The weapon's traverse range was also considered too small, and the targeting system was simply rudimentary.

The cockpit layout was also criticized. The crew's field of view was less than ideal. There was a shockingly large dead zone, which was caused by the fact that the gunner and pilot were positioned one behind the other, offset slightly to the side. This arrangement had been chosen to give the pilot a better view forward. It led, however, to a restricted view forward and to the right for the pilot and to the left for the gunner.

Although the cockpit had extensive glazing, the field of view was restricted by its numerous frames. As well, in sunlight there were numerous reflections on the glazing, which were distracting. In low-level flight the surface of the earth was sometimes reflected on the glazing, which irritated the crew.

In greater, more extended exposure to sunlight the cockpit became so hot that the pilots had the impression they were sitting in a greenhouse. It was not for nothing that they named the Mi-24A's cockpit the "veranda."

The major point of criticism in the cockpit, however, was the inadequate ballistic protection for the crew. The extensive glazing made the gunner and pilot feel as if they were sitting on a salver. In front they were protected by a not-particularly-large armor glass panel, but all of the other glazing was made of Plexiglas and offered no protection whatever against small-arms fire. The lower cockpit armor was considered adequate, but it did not extend upward far enough to give a true feeling of security.

In frontline service the Mi-24 revealed several technical weaknesses. The early-production engines had a limited operating life, being used up after 100 operating hours. Improved versions increased engine life to 300 and later 750 hours of operation.

Pilots continued to find that the tail rotor did not work effectively enough in some flight maneuvers. The problem appeared mainly in strong side winds, which negatively affected directional stability. The design of the tail boom was therefore changed and the tail rotor was relocated from the starboard to the port side. From there the tail rotor rotated up on the side toward the front of the aircraft, into the downwash of the rotor, improving its efficiency.

Mi-24As with the new tail rotor began leaving the production line in 1973. Mi-24As already in service were not modified, however.

The Americans had a similar problem with their AH-1G Cobras in Vietnam. Here, too, a change was made from a tractor to a thrust rotor by placing the tail rotor on the other side of the tail boom. The switch was made in exactly the opposite way on the Mi-24A, however. This was necessary because the tail rotors of the two helicopter types rotated in the opposite direction.

The Mi-24A was the first operational version. *Russkiye Vertolyoty*

Early in the Mi-24's service life, many pilots had to learn an unusual lesson. Until then, they had not flown aircraft with a retractable undercarriage, and occasionally they forgot to lower the wheels while on approach to land, which usually ended in a belly landing. But thanks to the helicopter's robust design, such incidents usually had no consequences that could not be overcome with the help of a crane.

This photo of an Mi-24A was taken by a member of the American Military Liaison Mission (MLM) near Retzov. It was the first time that an Mi-24A was photographically documented by a Westerner. *Bill Burhans, US MLM, US DoD*

The Mi-24A remained in service with the Soviet military for only a relatively short time. They were withdrawn from service as soon as more-modern versions became available, and were sold to Third World countries and subsequently served with the armed forces of Vietnam, Algeria, and Afghanistan. A very few examples made their way into museums.

The Mi-24A was the very first version of the Mi-24 to see combat. This took place in 1977, in the Ogaden War between Somalia and Ethiopia. In 1979, it saw action in the hands of the Vietnamese during the liberation of Cambodia from the tyranny of the Khmer Rouge and in defending against Chinese aggression, and that same year it took part in the occupation of Afghanistan by Soviet forces. NATO code-named the Mi-24A the Hind A.

The Mi-24A's cockpit was spacious, but only the small window in front of the gunner was protected by armor glass. *USMLM via www.16va.be*

The Mi-24A formed part of the equipment of the 16th Air Army of the Group of Soviet Forces in Germany. *Vladimir Sergeyev via www.16va.be*

This Mi-24 in Ukrainian markings is on display in a museum.

Mi-24U (*isdeliye 244*)

The Mi-24U (Ми-24У, Изделие 244) was the training variant derived from the Mi-24A. The suffix *U* stood for *uchebnui* (учебны), which translated means training or instruction.

The Mi-24U was used primarily for training helicopter pilots and carried none of the weapons served by the gunner of the Mi-24A. This meant that it was delivered without the nose-mounted machine gun and guided antitank missile capability. Weapons for which the pilot of the helicopter was responsible could however be carried on the stores racks on the stub wings. The Mi-24U was thus capable of employing unguided rockets, cannon pods, and bombs, but as a rule this was never practiced.

There were several differences in the cockpit of the Mi-24U compared to the Mi-24A, which were attributable to its role as a training Korolev.

Mi-24A Specifications

Measurements	
Rotor diameter	56.75 ft.
Fuselage length	57.4 ft.
Overall length	65 ft.
Wingspan	21.5 ft.
Height	14.6 ft.
Rotor circular area	2,530 sq. ft.
Number of rotor blades	five-blade main rotor / three-blade tail rotor
Weights	
Empty weight	19,125 lbs.
Takeoff weight	23,369 lbs.
Maximum takeoff weight	25,353 lbs.
Fuel capacity	561 gal. + two 215 gal. auxiliary tanks
Power Plants	two TV3-117 turboshafts
Takeoff power	2 × 1,972 hp
Performance	
Maximum speed	199 mph at 3,280 ft.
Cruise speed	174 mph
Range	301 mi.
Hover to altitude	5,249 ft.
Ceiling	16,732 ft.
Rate of climb	up to 41 ft./sec.
Armament	
Nose machine gun	one 12.7 mm MG A-12.7 with 700 rounds
Weapons stations	four UB-32, each with 32 S-5 rockets four bombs four Falanga-M guided antitank missiles
Payload	5,291 lbs. eight passengers
Crew	two or three

The forward position in the Mi-24U's cockpit was occupied by an instructor instead of a gunner. Unlike the Mi-24A, the Mi-24U's forward cockpit had full controls and a complete set of flight instruments.

The same position in the Mi-24A had only rudimentary equipment to enable the gunner to fly the aircraft in an emergency. The student pilot sat in the rear position, which was identical to that of the Mi-24A.

The Mi-24U underwent trials in 1972 and was produced in relatively small numbers from 1973 to 1974. NATO code-named the Mi-24U Hind C.

Mi-24B (*isdeliye* 241)

In many publications, one can read that the Mi-24B (Ми-24Б, Изделие 241) was another transitional variant. This is not quite so, however, since the Mi-24B was the first version of the attack helicopter as Mikhail Mil had envisaged it from the beginning. It finally had the long-awaited, rapid-firing Yak-B rotary machine gun and the Falanga-PV guided antitank missile complex.

The Falanga P was a major advance because compared to the previous version, it did not have to be guided manually, instead using a semiautomatic guidance system. The effectiveness of the guided antitank missile was still largely dependent on the ability of the gunner, but under ideal conditions, average accuracy improved from 30 to 80 percent.

Because the equipment needed to guide the guided antitank missile could not be housed completely in the helicopter's cockpit, the designers decided to place some of the equipment outside. This included the rotating antenna of the Raduga-F guidance system, which was housed in a teardrop-shaped housing beneath the port side of the nose, and the gyrostabilized optics with protective door housed in a fairing under the starboard nose. To give the additional fixtures sufficient ground clearance, it was necessary to lengthen the nosewheel leg.

The Mi-24B could easily be distinguished from the Mi-24A by its Yak-B 12.7 mm rapid-firing machine gun. The Yak-B was housed in a USPU-24 rotating chin turret and was operated by the gunner with the aid of the KPS-53AV (КПС-53АВ) targeting system. The weapon was aimed at the selected target on the basis of targeting instructions received from the SPSV-24 (СПСВ-24) analog computer after analysis of sensor information from the angle-of-attack indicator and pitot tube.

Mi-24U Specifications

Measurements	
Rotor diameter	56.75 ft.
Fuselage length	57.4 ft.
Overall length	65 ft.
Wingspan	21.5 ft.
Height	14.6 ft.
Rotor circular area	2,530 sq. ft.
Number of rotor blades	five-blade main rotor / three-blade tail rotor
Weights	
Empty weight	19,015 lbs.
Takeoff weight	23,369 lbs.
Maximum takeoff weight	25,353 lbs.
Fuel capacity	561 gal. + two 215 gal. auxiliary tanks
Power Plants	two TV3-117 turboshafts
Takeoff power	2 × 1,972 hp
Performance	
Maximum speed	199 mph at 3,280 ft.
Cruise speed	174 mph
Range	301 mi.
Hover to altitude	5,249 ft.
Ceiling	16,732 ft.
Rate of climb	up to 41 ft./sec.
Armament	
Nose machine gun	one 12.7 mm MG A-12.7 with 700 rounds
Weapons stations	four UB-32, each with 32 S-5 rockets four bombs
Payload	5,291 lbs. eight passengers
Crew	two

The prototypes of the Mi-24B underwent extensive testing in 1971 and 1972 and were assessed as clearly superior to the Mi-24A.

No large-scale production took place, however, because at that time the OKB Mil was engaged in redesigning the Mi-24's nose in order to achieve the improvements in ballistic defense for the crew, urgently requested by operational pilots.

The starting point of the redesign was the assessment that the original heavily glazed cockpit had serious shortcomings. Although the cockpit was rela-

This early Mi-24B has a single-barrel MG A-12.7 in a USPU-24 rotating turret. *OKB Mil*

This Mi-24B prototype is armed with the Yak-B 12.7 mm machine gun, four UB-32 rocket pods, and four Falanga-P guided antitank missiles. *OKB Mil*

tively spacious, blind spots made life difficult for the crew. The gunner blocked part of the pilot's field of view forward and to the right, while his view was restricted to the rear and to the left. The presence of both crew members in a single cockpit also brought with it the risk that both of them could be put out of action by a single hit in the cockpit area, resulting in the loss of the helicopter. The solution to this problem was seen to be separate, heavily armored cockpits. The cockpits were placed precisely on the helicopter's longitudinal axis, which improved the crew's view and reduced the blind spot considerably. The cockpits were now also staggered vertically, so that the pilot could easily see over the gunner. Both cockpits had a thick armor glass panel in front, which was capable of withstanding a direct hit from 12.7 mm weapons. The nose armor now extended to the crew's shoulders and provided very good protection against small-arms fire. Crew survivability was also improved by removing the ammunition for the nose machine gun from the cockpit. In the redesigned nose, ammunition for the machine gun was housed in a magazine below the right side of the cockpit.

In the early summer of 1972, two V-24 prototypes were fitted with the new nose section and underwent testing. It was envisaged that they would be equipped with the new Shturm guided antitank missile, which was expected to become available in 1973.

Since the combination of the Shturm-V and the redesigned nose promised a much-better attack helicopter than the Mi-24B could ever be, the Mi-24B never entered production. The OKB instead decided to put wood behind the arrow and immediately switch over to the third variant of the Mi-24. This variant was given the designation *isdeliye* 242 (Изделие 242). Mi-24V (Ми-24В) was the envisaged service designation (*V* is the third letter in the Cyrillic alphabet).

When in 1973 it became apparent that the Shturm-V would still not be ready to enter service, *isdeliye* 242 was temporarily put on ice and another interim version was envisaged. It was to have the redesigned nose and carry the weapons system of the Mi-24B. This variant was given the designation *isdeliye* 246. Test examples of *isdeliye* 246 were built from two Mi-24Bs (or Mi-24As, according to other sources). They were tested and received very good marks. In keeping with previous practice of naming versions of the Mi-24 after letters of the Cyrillic alphabet, *isdeliye* 246 should have been the Mi-24G (the fourth letter in the Cyrillic alphabet). They were anything but happy about the abbreviation G, however, because it was feared that the G would be taken to mean *govno*, a rather rude term in Russian soldiers' jargon. To avoid this fecal expression, the new attack helicopter was given the next letter in the Cyrillic alphabet and thus became the Mi-24D.

NATO issued no code name for the Mi-24B, because Western intelligence was unaware of its existence for a long time.

Mi-24D (*isdeliye* 246)

As previously mentioned several times, the Mi-24D, the next transitional version of Mil's attack helicopter, was essentially an emergency solution that was supposed to bridge the period until the Mi-24V became ready for service. However, like many provisional solutions before and after it, the Mi-24D was to prove much more durable than expected. It remained in production for ten years, with many of them being produced alongside its successor, the Mi-24V.

The Mi-24D was produced by combining the Mi-24B's weapons system with the modified helicopter airframe with the redesigned nose section. Tow prototypes were built in 1972 through the conversion of two earlier Mi-24Bs (or Mi-24As, according to other sources). The prototypes were very similar to the later production models, but they retained the old tail rotor layout with the rotor on the starboard side of the tail boom.

Flight testing of the Mi-24D began in the late summer of 1972, and continued until autumn 1974.

The helicopter factory in Arsenyev began production of the Mi-24D in 1973. For a time it was produced alongside the old Mi-24A. A short time

Mi-24B Specifications

Measurements	
Rotor diameter	56.75 ft.
Fuselage length	57.4 ft.
Overall length	65 ft.
Wingspan	21.5 ft.
Height	14.6 ft.
Rotor circular area	2,530 sq. ft.
Number of rotor blades	five-blade main rotor / three-blade tail rotor
Weights	
Empty weight	19,400 lbs.
Takeoff weight	24,250 lbs.
Maximum takeoff weight	25,353 lbs.
Fuel capacity	561 gal. + two 215 gal. auxiliary tanks
Power Plants	two TV3-117 turboshafts
Takeoff power	2 × 1,972 hp
Performance	
Maximum speed	199 mph at 3,280 ft.
Cruise speed	174 mph
Range	301 mi.
Hover to altitude	5,249 ft.
Ceiling	16,732 ft.
Rate of climb	up to 41 ft./sec.
Armament	
Revolving turret	one 12.7 mm Yak-B with 1,470 rounds
Weapons stations	four UB-32, each with thirty-two S-5 rockets four bombs four Falanga-P guided antitank missiles
Payload	5,291 lbs. eight passengers
Crew	two or three

later, Helicopter Factory No. 168 in Rostov on Don also began mass production. Production at Arsenyev continued until 1977. After about 350 units, the factory switched production to the Mi-24V. At Rostov on Don, production of the Mi-24D continued until 1983 (or 1986, according to other sources). Production there concentrated on Mi-24Ds destined for export.

Except for a few details, the Mi-24Ds exported to nations of the Warsaw Pact were identical to those produced for the Soviet military. A "refined," or simplified,

The first Mi-24Ds were delivered without dust covers in front of the engine intakes. *OKB Mil*

version was delivered to "friendly states" that were not members of the Warsaw Pact, as the Mi-25.

Interestingly, the Mi-24D was denied official acceptance into the Soviet armed services for a long time, even though quantity production was in full swing and the frontline units were rapidly equipping with the new Mi-24 variant. Official acceptance did not take place until March 29, 1976, the same day the Mi-24V officially entered service with the Soviet air force. It can be assumed that the reason for this approach was an attempt to maintain the alphabetical sequence (*V* is the third letter of the Cyrillic alphabet. For aesthetic reasons the fourth letter, *G*, was omitted, and *D* is the fifth letter).

By that time about 200 examples of the Mi-24D were in service.

During its operational life the Mi-24D underwent continual improvement. In 1975, dust covers were introduced in front of the air intakes to prevent foreign-object damage (FOD) to the engines. The third series of the TV3-117 engine was introduced in 1977. This engine had a longer operating life and improved operating reliability. The last Mi-24Ds built for export in the 1980s were fitted with more-powerful TV3-117V engines.

In 1980, the Mi-24D took part in the Soviet invasion of Afghanistan. The resulting ten-year war was a difficult test for the helicopter. The Mi-24D was highly regarded by the Soviet units fighting there, on account of its ability to stand up under fire and its overwhelming firepower. The units nicknamed the helicopter "Crocodile." Often the mere appearance of the "Crocodiles" was sufficient to force the enemy onto the defensive. The Mi-24D was feared and hated by the enemy, the *dushmani* or *mujahideen*. The Mi-24D had little to fear from small-arms fire unless it came under fire from the side, where the cockpit was vulnerable. This did not change until the Western states began supplying the rebels with shoulder-fired surface-to-air missiles, or man-portable air defense systems (MANPADS). For a certain time the Soviet helicopter forces were paralyzed and losses rose significantly, but this success was of a temporary nature.

To counter the threat from infrared-guided missiles, the Mi-24D was fitted initially with two but later four flare dispensers. The flare dispensers were attached to the tail boom with tension bands, and the control units were installed in the cockpit. In the mid-1980s the Lipa (Ispanka) infrared jammer also entered service.

An updated Polish
Mi-24D in high-speed,
low-level flight. *Rocha*

The "horns" on
both sides of the
cockpit indicate
that this Mi-24D
was retrofitted
with a modern
radar-warning
system. *Scheffler
Collection*

29

Poland used the Mi-24D during the ISAF mission in Afghanistan. Note the eyes painted on the dust covers in front of the engine intakes, the retrofitted Ispanka infrared jammer, and the flare dispenser under the tail boom. *US DoD*

This NVA Mi-24D is now on display at the Cottbus airfield museum. In the background is an Mi-9. *Normann*

The Mi-24D proved itself well during the conflict in Afghanistan. It was robust and resistant to enemy fire, but it displayed weaknesses in high-altitude flight. Its service ceiling was so low that it could not fly over the high mountain ranges. The crews were therefore forced to fly in the valleys, which resulted in detours and lost time and exposed them to enemy fire. The available weapons spectrum also proved less effective than desired.

In central Europe, where the Mi-24D represented the bulk of the Warsaw Pact states' helicopter forces, by the mid-1980s it began to become obsolescent. The Falanga P guided antitank missile was not capable of penetrating the frontal armor of the latest generation of NATO tanks. At the end of the 1980s, therefore, efforts were made to update the Mi-24D to Mi-24V standard. In the German Democratic Republic this modernization was envisaged for the early 1990s. The delivery of a single Mi-24V was conceived for 1990 to serve as a pattern aircraft for the future modernization.

At the urging of West German advisors, the new East German government elected in 1990 canceled this order and was forced to pay a considerable contract penalty to the manufacturer.

The Mi-24Ds of the NVA (National Peoples Army) were initially absorbed by the *Bundeswehr* and were kept in limited operation until 1993. After that, the helicopters were given to other countries or retired.

The Mi-24D or Mi-25 was exported in large numbers. In addition to the war in Afghanistan, its most important use was in the war in Lebanon in 1982, where a handful of Syrian Mi-25s destroyed more than ninety Israeli vehicles, including examples of the modern and very well-protected Merkava battle tank. In Angola and Mozambique, government troops used the Mi-25 against rebel groups controlled by South Africa. In service with Sandinista Nicaragua, the Mi-25 was used

Mi-24D Specifications

Measurements	
Rotor diameter	56.75 ft.
Fuselage length	57.4 ft.
Overall length	65 ft.
Wingspan	21.5 ft.
Height	14.6 ft.
Rotor circular area	2,530 sq. ft.
Number of rotor blades	five-blade main rotor / three-blade tail rotor
Weights	
Empty weight	18,629 lbs.
Takeoff weight	24,691 lbs.
Maximum takeoff weight	25,353 lbs.
Fuel capacity	561 gal. + two 215 gal. auxiliary tanks
Power Plants	
	two TV3-117 third-series turboshafts
Takeoff power	2 × 2,200 hp
Performance	
Maximum speed	199 mph at 3,280 ft.
Cruise speed	161 mph
Range	310 to 466 mi.
Hover to altitude	4,265 ft.
Ceiling	14,764 ft.
Rate of climb	up to 41 ft./sec.
Armament	
Revolving turret	one 12.7 mm Yak-B with 1,470 rounds
Weapons stations	four UB-32, each with 32 57-mm rockets four bombs four Falanga-P guided antitank missiles
Payload	5,291 lbs. eight passengers
Crew	two or three

to combat contra rebels financed and equipped by the United States. Gaddafi used the Mi-25 in his military adventures in Chad, and Saddam Hussein sent his Mi-25s into the field in the war with Iran.

NATO had great respect for the Mi-24D and assigned it the code name Hind D.

Mi-24DU (*isdeliye* 249)

The training variant derived from the Mi-24D was designated Mi-24DU (Ми-24ДУ, Изделие 249). It began leaving the production line in 1980 and was used to train helicopter pilots to fly all subsequent versions of the Mi-24, since there were no training variants of the Mi-24V and Mi-24P.

Unlike the combat version, the Mi-24DU had no machine gun armament and was also not equipped to use guided antitank missiles. The flight instructor sat in the front cockpit of the Mi-24DU, which had a complete set of flight controls plus flight and navigation systems. The student pilot sat in the rear cockpit, which was identical to that of an Mi-24 combat version. The Mi-24DU was offered for export as the Mi-25U.

Mi-24V (*isdeliye* 242)

From the beginning, the Soviet military insisted that the newly developed Shturm-V guided antitank missile should be used with the Mi-24 helicopter. One of the first V-24 prototypes built in Arsenyev was prepared and used specifically for testing of this weapon. Despite all efforts, the guided antitank missile could not be made ready for service in time, resulting, as previously mentioned, in the need to create several interim versions of the Mi-24.

After evaluating initial operational experience, in 1972 a new cockpit section was designed for the Mi-24, which was tested in 1973. The new forward section proved a great success and received unanimous approval from the test pilots. All future versions of the Mi-24 would be equipped with it, above all the Mi-24V destined for the Shturm guided antitank missile.

It was anticipated that the missile would become operational in 1973. This target date could not be met, however, and the Mi-24D was created as an interim variant.

One of the first Mi-24D production aircraft was used for further testing of the Shturm guided antitank missile, however, and took over the role of the V-24 prototype. Testing of the new weapons system using the Mi-24V prototype began in 1973 and was completed in 1975. After the conclusion of state trials, production began in the factories at Arsenyev and Rostov on Don.

Mi-24DU Specifications

Measurements	
Rotor diameter	56.75 ft.
Fuselage length	57.4 ft.
Overall length	65 ft.
Wingspan	21.5 ft.
Height	14.6 ft.
Rotor circular area	2,530 sq. ft.
Number of rotor blades	five-blade main rotor / three-blade tail rotor
Weights	
Empty weight	18,519 lbs.
Takeoff weight	24,471 lbs.
Maximum takeoff weight	25,353 lbs.
Fuel capacity	561 gal. + two 215 gal. auxiliary tanks
Power Plants	
	two TV3-117 third-series turboshafts
Takeoff power	2 × 2,200 hp
Performance	
Maximum speed	199 mph at 3,280 ft.
Cruise speed	161 mph
Range	310 to 466 mi.
Hover to altitude	4,265 ft.
Ceiling	14,764 ft.
Rate of climb	up to 41 ft./sec.
Armament	
Revolving turret	one 12.7 mm Yak-B with 1,470 rounds
Weapons stations	four UB-32, each with thirty-two 57 mm rockets four bombs
Payload	5,291 lbs. eight passengers
Crew	two or three

The Mi-24V was accepted into the Soviet armed forces on March 29, 1976, the same day as the Mi-24D.

Externally, the first Mi-24Vs differed little from the Mi-24D. Under the skin, much of the aircraft's equipment also remained the same. Essentially the only difference was replacement of the former Falanga-P main weapons system with the clearly more modern Shturm V supersonic guided antitank missile. The launch equipment on the wingtip pylons on the stub wings had also been reworked. The outer underwing pylons could now also be fitted with twin launchers for guided antitank missiles, which increased the total number of missiles that could be carried to eight.

The previously used Raduga-F guidance system was replaced by the new Raduga-Sh, which had been developed specially for the Shturm V missile. It was incapable, however, of guiding the older missile systems.

Another difference from the Mi-24D was the Mi-24V's ability to carry fuel tanks on its underwing pylons. This made it possible to do away with the auxiliary tanks usually installed in the cargo compartment for ferry flights and to instead transport items of equipment, spare parts, or personnel. The installation of internal auxiliary fuel tanks in the cargo compartment is still possible, however.

Thanks to its modern guided-weapons system, in tactical terms the Mi-24V was clearly superior to the Mi-24D. In aeronautical terms, however, the two versions were almost identical, because the machines had roughly the same takeoff weight and were equipped with the same engines from the third series of the TV3-117.

This changed in 1980 with the start of the war in Afghanistan. In the very first weeks of the war, the pilots realized that the Mi-24's high-altitude performance was inadequate. The helicopter had been designed for use over the flat plains of central Europe, a potential theater of war full of antiaircraft weapons. Since an attack helicopter could survive in such an

Essentially the only difforonco between the early Mi-24V and the Mi-24D was the Shturm-V guided antitank missile system. *OKB Mil*

An updated Mi-24V during takeoff. Flare dispensers, an infrared jammer, and SPO-15 radar-warning receiver have been retrofitted to the helicopter. *Butowski via Rostvertol PLC*

environment only by operating at extremely low level, the Mi-24 was optimized for precisely that operational scenario. In the mountains of Afghanistan, however, it was required to fly at great heights, which was impossible with the existing engines.

The TV3-117V engine variant optimized for high-altitude performance was therefore created in 1980 and put into production. Henceforth all Mi-24Vs destined for Afghanistan were fitted with this engine, while the rest had to get by with the TV3-117 of the third series. After the expansion of engine production, all new-build Mi-24Vs received the TV3-117V. In 1986, the further-improved TV3-117VM and TV3-117VMA were also introduced.

The Mi-24V underwent a constant modification and improvement program. Its weapons array was expanded in keeping with wartime experience. Larger unguided rockets, area weapons systems, and new cannon pods were made available and a laser rangefinder was added.

In 1986, OKB Mil tested quadruple launchers for the Shturm-V guided antitank missile. The total number of available guided weapons thus rose to sixteen. Initially this configuration was not used in service. It first saw service later on modernization versions of the Mi-24.

In the mid-1980s the previous radar-warning receiver was replaced by the modern SPO-15 receiver. This warning receiver not only indicated an illuminating radar's direction of origin more precisely than the previous model, it was also capable of determining whether the illumination was coming from above, below, or the same height. It could indicate the strength of the radar and also give a hint as to what threat category the emitting radar fell. Mi-24s thus equipped could be identified by the hornlike receiving antenna near the aft cockpit.

With the appearance of portable surface-to-air missiles, the Mi-24 was equipped with defense and protection mechanisms. At first this was accomplished by attaching flare dispensers to the tail boom with tension bands. At first, two dispensers, one on each side, were mounted. This number was later increased to four. The corresponding control elements were retrofitted in the cockpit.

On new-production Mi-24Vs, three flare dispensers were fitted on each side of the fuselage, first without and then with aerodynamic fairings.

The principal means of defense against portable surface-to-air missiles was the Lipa (Ispanka) infrared-jamming device. It was retrofitted to Mi-24Vs already in service and installed at the factory on new aircraft.

This Czech Mi-24V is armed with 23 mm cannon pods and Shturm-V guided antitank missiles. *Shaposhnikova Rostvertol PLC*

Beginning in 1984, production engines were modified so that the AVU (ЭВУ) infrared suppressor system could be installed. AVU screened the direct view of the hot engine exhausts and directed the gases upward into the rotor stream, where they were swirled and cooled. On its own, AVU was effective only against first-generation missiles such as the Redeye and Strela 2. Against modern missiles such as the FIM-92A Stinger, it was not effective enough. In conjunction with flares and the LIPA infrared jammer, however, it was able to improve the Mi-24V's survivability significantly.

Further modifications, such as improved armor protection for the cockpit, were carried out until production stopped in 1989.

The Mi-24V was the most widely used version of the Mi-24. More than 1,500 examples of this subtype were built in both factories. Various operators also updated their Mi-24Ds to Mi-24V standard.

The Mi-24V remains in use to the present day and in many countries forms the backbone of their helicopter units, as for example in Poland and the Czech Republic.

The Mi-35, a simplified export version, was offered to nations outside the Warsaw Pact. It was procured by India, Syria, Libya, and Iraq, among others.

A training variant analogous to the Mi-24DU and Mi-25U was provided to India; however, this training version was not given a special variant designation.

The Mi-24V received its baptism of fire in Afghanistan. It was not until after the fall of the Soviet Union that it saw action in further conflicts, such as in Croatia and Macedonia. The Mi-35 export variant, however, had already seen action in the Iran-Iraq war and confrontations between India and Pakistan. Hind E was the NATO code name for the Mi-24V.

The front end of a Czech Mi-24V. Visible here are the housings for the AVU self-defense system on front of the engine air intakes, and the radar-warning system's hornlike antennas abeam the pilot's cockpit. *Normann*

Polish Mi-24V during the ISAF mission in Afghanistan. *US Army, Jim Hinnant*

Mi-24Vs displayed at airshows often wear colorful special finishes, such as here at ILA 2014. *Normann*

Mi-24V Specifications

Measurements	
Rotor diameter	56.75 ft.
Fuselage length	57.4 ft.
Overall length	65 ft.
Wingspan	21.5 ft.
Height	14.6 ft.
Rotor circular area	2,530 sq. ft.
Number of rotor blades	five-blade main rotor / three-blade tail rotor

Weights	
Empty weight	19,004 lbs.
Takeoff weight	24,691 lbs.
Maximum takeoff weight	25,353 lbs.
Fuel capacity	561 gal. + four 112 gal. auxiliary tanks

Power Plants	two TV3-117V turboshafts
Takeoff power	2 × 2,073 hp (to 2,762 hp)

Performance	
Maximum speed	205 mph at 3,280 ft.
Cruise speed	161 mph
Range	310 to 621 mi.
Hover to altitude	7,218 ft.
Ceiling	15,091 ft.
Rate of climb	up to 41 ft. / sec.

Armament	
Revolving turret	one 12.7 mm Yak-B with 1,470 rounds
Weapons stations	four UB-32, each with thirty-two 57 mm rockets four B-8, each with twenty 80 mm rockets four bombs or cluster bombs Two cannon pods eight Shturm-V guided antitank missiles
Payload	5,291 lbs. eight passengers
Crew	two or three

Hungary Airshow 2007. *József Süveg*

Another colorful Czech Mi-24. *Johan Wieland*

Mi-24P (isdeliye 243)

The development of the BMP-1 armored personnel carrier by the Soviet side led to a counterreaction by NATO, which was to build better-armored combat vehicles for transporting personnel. The result was the Marder in Germany and the AMX-10P in France, while the Americans developed the XM273, which many years later was to become the M2 Bradley.

OKB Mil had suspected since the mid-1970s that in the future the firepower of the 12.7 mm machine gun would no longer be sufficient to defeat opposing armored personnel carriers. A cannon with greater penetrative power was urgently required. There were weapons available in calibers of 23 and 30 mm. The developers of the OKB Mil voted for the 23 mm GSh-

23 cannon; however, the military insisted on a 30 mm weapon, which to the military bureaucrats seemed to be an optimal choice of caliber for use by all branches of the military. At that time in the Soviet Union, efforts were underway to simplify the logistics of ammunition provisioning, in which all weapons with a caliber of 30 mm were supposed to be designed for a new standard shell. Whether the cannon was to be installed in a combat aircraft, helicopter, antiaircraft system, or warship, the ammunition would be the same everywhere, and supplying the troops would be simpler to manage than with the until-then-standard confusion of different shells for one and the same caliber.

Forward view of the Mi-24P. Ablogin via Rostvertol

Mi-24Ps of the Russian Berkuty Display team taking off. *Ablogin via Rostvertol*

In keeping with the caliber specified by the military, the twin-barreled GSh-30-2 cannon (alias GSh-2-30, alias GSh-302, alias GSh-302) was chosen for the cannon-armed variant of the Mi-24. It was based on the widely used, tried and reliable GSh-23, which led the Moscow helicopter developer to rightly assume that the 30 mm cannon would have inherited the positive characteristics of its predecessor.

Preliminary work on the project began in 1974, and the GSh-30-2 was installed in an Mi-24 for the first time in 1975. An Mi-24V prototype from which the Yak-B machine gun had been removed served as the test aircraft. Installation of the GSh-30-2 in a revolving turret was not possible because of its weight and the anticipated heavy recoil of the automatic cannon. The weapon was therefore installed rigidly on the longitudinal axis, directly above the ammunition magazine located on the starboard side of the fuselage. Thus modified, the aircraft was given the designation Mi-24P (*isdeliye* 243) (Ми-24П, Изделие 243). The *P* stood for *pushka* (пушка), meaning cannon, but could also be understood as *pushetshni* (пушечный) or cannon armed.

During testing of this weapons system, the developer ran into a series of unexpected problems.

The muzzle pressure of the GSh-30-2 was so great that it damaged the Mi-24P's external skinning. The weapon's muzzles were so unfortunately placed that the bright muzzle flashes blinded the gunner and pilot, which represented a serious problem especially at night and in twilight. The heavy vibrations that resulted when the weapon was fired caused electronic components to fail regularly, and to top it off, the weapon's penetrative power proved to be far less than expected.

Mi-24P Specifications

Measurements	
Rotor diameter	56.75 ft.
Fuselage length	57.4 ft.
Overall length	65 ft.
Wingspan	21.5 ft.
Height	14.6 ft.
Rotor circular area	2,530 sq. ft.
Number of rotor blades	five-blade main rotor / three-blade tail rotor

Weights	
Empty weight	18,893 lbs.
Takeoff weight	24,912 lbs.
Maximum takeoff weight	26,015 lbs.
Fuel capacity	561 gal. + four 112 gal. auxiliary tanks

Power Plants	two TV3-117V turboshafts
Takeoff power	2 x 2,073 hp (to 2,762 hp)

Performance	
Maximum speed	205 mph at 3,280 ft.
Cruise speed	161 mph
Range	310 to 621 mi.
Hover to altitude	6,561 ft.
Ceiling	14,763 ft.
Rate of climb	up to 41 ft./sec.

Armament	
Revolving turret	one GSh-30-2K with 250 rounds
Weapons stations	four UB-32, each with thirty-two 57 mm rockets four B-8, each with twenty 80 mm rockets four bombs or cluster bombs two cannon pods eight Shturm-V guided antitank missiles
Payload	5,291 lbs. eight passengers
Crew	two or three

In its early days, Berkuty, the Russian helicopter display team, flew standard-production Mi-24Ps. *Micheyev via Rostvertol PLC*

The last point was noticed with astonishment, since the same weapon was used in the Sukhoi T-8 close-support aircraft, the later Su-25, and no problems with its penetrative ability had arisen. The solution to the mystery lay in the fact that the T-8's speed while approaching the target was much higher than that of

An Mi-24P of the Russian armed forces. *Butowski via Rostvertol PLC*

an Mi-24P. Since the aircraft's own speed added to the weapon's muzzle velocity, a shell fired by a T-8 flying at 447 mph had a velocity 120 mph, greater than a shell fired from a hovering Mi-24P. Penetrative ability varied accordingly.

To give the Mi-24P the necessary penetrative capability, it was necessary to improve the automatic cannon's performance. Representatives of the OKB Mil contacted the weapons maker in Tula and spoke

to its chief designer, Gryasev. It was decided to lengthen the weapon's barrel by about 3.3 feet.

Work to modify the cannon lasted several years, and when the weapon, now designated GSh-30-2K, was ready for service it took considerable time until the problem of the powerful vibration could be solved.

State testing of the Mi-24P was completed successfully in 1980. This version began leaving the production halls of both Mi-24 manufacturers in

For a long time, the Mi-24P was the backbone of the Russian attack helicopter units. *Soldatkin via Rostvertol*

The Mi-24P was used in the Caucasus during the war in Chechnya. *Russian Ministry of Defense*

This Mi-24P is carrying external fuel tanks for increased range. *Romanenko via Rostvertol*

1981. By the time production ended in 1989, 623 examples of this type had been completed.

Like the Mi-24V, which was built in parallel and was identical apart from the Mi-24P's cannon armament, it underwent a similar constant development process.

The first Mi-24Ps were still powered by TV3-117 engines from the third production series. All the Mi-24Ps destined for Afghanistan soon received the TV3-117V, and, from 1986 onward, the TV3-117VMA. The new engines were later used in all Mi-24Ps.

The Mi-24P also initially had no protective equipment against infrared-guided missiles. Flare dispensers were retrofitted during the Afghanistan war and were attached beneath the tail boom with

Cyprus procured
new Mi-35P
helicopters.
They have a fixed
undercarriage
and shortened
stub wings.
Rostvertol PLC

Peru received updated Mi-35P attack helicopters. *Romanenko via Rostvertol*

This Russian Mi-24P is wearing a modern gray camouflage finish. *Romanenko via Rostvertol*

tension bands. The Mi-24P was later fitted at the factory with three flare dispensers on each side of the fuselage. The dispensers were initially simply screwed onto the fuselage, but later they were covered by an aerodynamic fairing.

As of 1984, all new-build Mi-24Ps were given the capability of carrying the AVU exhaust gas–cooling system. The Lipa (Ispanka) infrared jammer was retrofitted and later installed at the factory.

A simplified version of the Mi-24P was offered in the nonsocialist economic zone as the Mi-35P.

The Mi-24P proved to be a very usable attack helicopter and is still in service worldwide. In recent years the Mi-24P has fought on the African continent, has borne the main burden of the fighting in the Donbas, and in 2015 was used by Russian units in Syria to protect their military bases there.

After a lengthy pause during which only the Mi-24P underwent combat capability improvements, in 2009 the Rostvertol helicopter factory in Rostov on Don resumed production. Many construction elements developed for the Mi-28 were integrated into the new-build Mi-24P or Mi-35P. The NATO code name for the Mi-24P is Hind F.

Mi-24RKhR (isdeliye 2462)

The Mi-24RKhR* (Ми-24PXP) was a highly specialized variant derived from the Mi-24V that was created for NBC reconnaissance (NBC stands for nuclear,

biological, chemical). For reasons of simplification, this variant was designated Mi-24R. This was a little misleading because the letter *R* as a rule stood for *rasvyedtchik* (разведчик), or reconnaissance aircraft. The RKhR was not a reconnaissance aircraft in the usual sense; instead it was a highly specialized chemical reconnaissance machine.

For this task it was equipped with devices for collecting and analyzing air and soil samples. The most noticeable of these installations were the small grab dredgers on the outer pylons, which replaced the usual guided antitank missile launch rails. With their help the chemical reconnaissance specialists could take soil samples without having to leave the protection of the helicopter. The air scoops on the port side of the fuselage below the cargo compartment, with which air samples could be gathered, were another easily identifiable feature.

Inside the freight compartment there were two work stations for ABC reconnaissance specialists, where the collected samples were tested for radioactive, chemical, or biological traces. The examination results could be sent to a ground station by a data transmission system.

To protect the crew and the reconnaissance specialists, the crew cabins and freight compartment were given improved protection against radioactivity as well as chemical and biological agents.

The prototype of the Mi-24RKhR was produced at the end of 1978, whereas the type was produced from 1983 to 1989. Depending on the source, production totaled 110, 152, or 160 Mi-24RKhRs.

* In English-language literature, the Cyrillic letter *X* is translated with the abbreviation *Kh*. The German transcription is *Cha*, with the *Ch* having a guttural pronunciation as in the word *suchen*.

Mi-24RKhR NBC reconnaissance helicopter, alias Mi-24R. *Mambour*

Mi-24RKhR Specifications

Measurements	
Rotor diameter	56.75 ft.
Fuselage length	57.4 ft.
Overall length	65 ft.
Wingspan	21.5 ft.
Height	14.6 ft.
Rotor circular area	2,530 sq. ft.
Number of rotor blades	five-blade main rotor / three-blade tail rotor
Weights	
Empty weight	18,850 lbs.
Takeoff weight	24,692 lbs.
Maximum takeoff weight	25,353 lbs.
Fuel capacity	561 gal. + four 112 gal. auxiliary tanks
Power Plants	two TV3-117V turboshafts
Takeoff power	2 × 2,073 hp (to 2,762 hp)
Performance	
Maximum speed	205 mph at 3,280 ft.
Cruise speed	161 mph
Range	310 to 621 mi.
Hover to altitude	6,561 ft.
Ceiling	15,092 ft.
Rate of climb	up to 41 ft./sec.
Armament	
Revolving turret	one 12.7-mm Yak-B with 1,470 rounds
Weapons stations	four UB-32, each with thirty-two 57 mm rockets four B-8, each with twenty 80 mm rockets four bombs or cluster bombs two cannon pods
Payload	NBC analysis laboratory two specialists
Crew	two

Claws for taking soil samples. *Mambour*

Intake for collecting air samples. *Mambour*

In 1986, Mi-24RKhR helicopters were used in response to the nuclear-reactor catastrophe at Chernobyl. They regularly flew over the destroyed reactor building and collected air and soil samples. Since radiation levels were very high, the crews of the Mi-24RKhR were pulled out during the course of the mission. The new crews were brought in from every Mi-24 unit in the USSR, some even from Afghanistan, for use at Chernobyl.

In 1995, the Mi-24RA, a developed version of the Mi-24RKhR, was tested in Russia. It was equipped with improved analytical technology, requiring just a single specialist to be carried. The NATO code name for the Mi-24RKhR was Hind G1.

Mi-24K (*isdeliye* 201)

The Mi-24K (Ми-24К Изделие 201) was a highly specialized subvariant of the Mi-24V.

It was supposed to fly over the battlefield as a flying artillery control point, seeking out enemy units, observing and assessing artillery and rocket fire by friendly units, and, if necessary, providing the necessary data for corrections. It was equipped with a highly developed optical sensor system, which was placed beneath the nose in place of the Raduga, the guided antitank missile guidance optics, and a powerful reconnaissance camera in the freight compartment.

The optical sensor system, which had the sonorous designation Iris (Ирис), was equipped with a swiveling wide-angle lens. It was served by an operator from the forward cockpit position. Iris was part of the Ruta (Рута) reconnaissance package, which also included an optical target identification system and a digital computer. According to several sources, the data could be transmitted by data link to a ground station in real time. Ultimately, storage media were present on the Mi-24K to save the collected data.

Mi-24K during preflight. *Mambour*

The Iris wide-angle optical sensor, here covered by a protective cover, enabled precise battlefield observation. *Mambour*

Mi-24K Specifications

Measurements	
Rotor diameter	56.75 ft.
Fuselage length	57.4 ft.
Overall length	65 ft.
Wingspan	21.5 ft.
Height	14.6 ft.
Rotor circular area	2,530 sq. ft.
Number of rotor blades	five-blade main rotor / three-blade tail rotor
Weights	
Empty weight	18,959 lbs.
Takeoff weight	24,692 lbs.
Maximum takeoff weight	25,353 lbs.
Fuel capacity	561 gal. + four 112 gal. auxiliary tanks
Power Plants	two TV3-117V turboshafts
Takeoff power	2 × 2,073 hp (to 2,762 hp)
Performance	
Maximum speed	205 mph at 3,280 ft.
Cruise speed	161 mph
Range	310 to 621 mi.
Hover to altitude	6,561 ft.
Ceiling	15,091 ft.
Rate of climb	up to 41 ft./sec.
Armament	
Revolving turret	one 12.7-mm Yak-B with 1,470 rounds
Weapons stations	four UB-32, each with thirty-two 57 mm rockets four B-8, each with twenty 80 mm rockets four bombs or cluster bombs two cannon pods
Payload	AFA-100 reconnaissance camera two specialists
Crew	two

An AFA-100 wide-aperture reconnaissance camera with a long focal length (f8 / 1,300 mm) was placed in a fixed installation in the right side of the fuselage. The large window for the camera lens on that side was a sure recognition feature of the Mi-24K.

The Mi-24K's armaments was similar to that of the Mi-24V, but they were reduced in the ability to use guided antitank missiles.

The first Mi-24K prototype was built in 1979, and the variant entered production in 1983. How many Mi-24Ks were built, by the time production ended in 1989, is not certain. Depending on the source, the numbers vary from 92 to 163 to 180 examples.

NATO gave the Mi-24K the code name Hind G2. In the Soviet military the letter *K* indicated *korrektirovshchik* (корректировщик), meaning corrector or artillery observer.

Mi-24VP (*isdeliye* 258)

During the war in Afghanistan it was found that the 12.7 mm rotary machine gun did not always work reliably. Alternatives to replace this weapon were therefore investigated. The 30 mm GSh-30-2 cannon tested on the Mi-24P could not be used in a revolving chin turret because it was too large and produced too much recoil.

Experience in Afghanistan with the GSh-30-2K in a fixed installation had also shown that a 30 mm weapon was often too large for engaging soft or lightly armored targets. The way out was to select a weapon

Mi-24VP Specifications

Measurements	
Rotor diameter	56.75 ft.
Fuselage length	57.4 ft.
Overall length	65 ft.
Wingspan	21.5 ft.
Height	14.6 ft.
Rotor circular area	2,530 sq. ft.
Number of rotor blades	five-blade main rotor / three-blade tail rotor
Weights	
Empty weight	18,739 lbs.
Takeoff weight	24,692 lbs.
Maximum takeoff weight	25,353 lbs.
Fuel capacity	561 gal. + four 112 gal. auxiliary tanks
Power Plants	two TV3-117V turboshafts
Takeoff power	2 × 2,073 hp (to 2,762 hp)
Performance	
Maximum speed	199 mph at 3,280 ft.
Cruise speed	168 mph
Range	280 to 621 mi.
Hover to altitude	6,561 ft.
Ceiling	15,092 ft.
Rate of climb	up to 41 ft./sec.
Armament	
Revolving turret	one GSh-23L with 450 rounds
Weapons stations	four UB-32, each with thirty-two 57 mm rockets four B-8, each with twenty 80 mm rockets four bombs or cluster bombs two cannon pods eight Shturm-V guided antitank missiles
Payload	5,291 lbs. eight passengers
Crew	two or three

with a caliber somewhere between 12.7 and 30 mm. And this weapon was the GSh-23L, a cannon that Mil had favored during the Mi-24 project phase. In the 1980s, the successor to Mil finally got the opportunity to use this weapon in the Mi-24.

A number of changes to the nose were necessary to accommodate the GSh-23L—an accurate and reliable cannon used in fighter aircraft—in the Mi-24V.

Frame 1N had to be reinforced to be able to take the greater forces of the new twin-barrel weapon. A new remotely controlled revolving turret also had to be developed, which was given the designation NPPU-24 (НППУ-24). It was envisaged to accept the air-cooled GSh-23L; a derivative was designated the

NPPU-23. This variant was designed for a water-cooled GSh-23V.

The Mi-24VP's ammunition capacity was 450 rounds. All other weapons options were equivalent to those of an Mi-24V produced at the end of the 1980s.

Mi-24VP of the Russian Baltic Fleet. *Micheyev*

The Mi-24PS was created by converting military machines. *Scheffler Collection*

The first Mi-24VP prototype was built in 1985. Because of the sharply rising economic crisis in the time of perestroika and glasnost, production of the Mi-24VP did not begin until 1989. About twenty-five machines were produced, which entered service with the Baltic Red Banner Fleet. That same year, however, production was halted for financial reasons.

Despite this failure, the Mi-24VP formed the starting point for further development of the Mi-24. From it, after the economic consolidation of Russia, came the dramatically modernized Mi-24VM, which today is produced as the Mi-35 at Rostov on Don and is exported worldwide. The NATO code name for the Mi-24VP is Hind H.

The Mi-24VP is still in service with Russia's Baltic Fleet. In 2016, it was observed in the area of Kaliningrad, the former Königsberg.

Mi-24PS

The Mi-24PS was a special version for the Russian Ministry of the Interior. The abbreviation *PS* stands for *patrulno-spasatelniy*, which literally translates as "search and rescue" or SAR.

The first prototype of the Mi-24PS was created in 1995 by converting a standard Mi-24P, which was completely demilitarized. A second prototype was derived from an Mi-24V.

Identifying features of this helicopter variant include extremely short stub wings with just one pylon for carrying external fuel tanks, several powerful loudspeakers on the aircraft's nose, and the absence of any weaponry. The Mi-24's military target search optics and fire-control system were replaced by modern civilian optics. The military communications system was also replaced by a civilian system.

The installation of a powerful searchlight and the presence of winches were indispensable for search-and-rescue missions. Additional handholds were mounted on the helicopter's airframe, which made it capable of rappelling four persons simultaneously.

Inside the cargo hold are six relatively comfortable seats for accompanying policemen.

The Mi-24PS helicopters are painted white and on their tail booms bear the word "militia."

Mi-24PN

From the beginning, the Mi-24 was characterized as an all-weather and night-capable combat aircraft. Compared to Western helicopters of the late 1980s, however, its night combat capabilities were definitely rather rudimentary. This problem was recognized during the Afghanistan war, and in the mid-1980s the Soviet Union launched developments aimed at closing the gap in night vision technology.

The collapse of the USSR and the chaos of the years that followed made it impossible to put modernization plans into practice. Not until 2000 had Russia stabilized sufficiently for sufficient funds to be made available for a targeted further development of the Mi-24.

The Mi-24PN was an interim night-combat-capable variant that incorporated numerous innovations, the most important of which was the integration of the Saryevo (Зарево) night vision system, which was fully stabilized and included a laser rangefinder. Saryevo was a development of the Noktyurn (Ноктюрн) thermal imaging device, which had its origins in tank construction. It was originally planned to integrate this device in an external pod and carry it on a wing pylon. This option was rejected, however, because the pod would have blocked a valuable weapons station. In addition, the night vision device's field of view to the side was of course restricted by the helicopter's fuselage.

It was therefore decided to install the Saryevo night vision system in the helicopter's nose. This led to the Mi-24PN's unmistakable pointed nose.

To further improve the helicopter's night combat capabilities, the cockpit of the Mi-24PN was designed for use of the ONV-1 Skolosk (ОНВ-1 "Скосок") night vision goggles. With the help of the night vision goggles it was possible to carry out nocturnal terrain-following flights to a minimum height of 160 feet above the ground. So that the night vision goggles could be used, the cockpit indicators had to be modified so that they did not blind the pilot. There were also some improvements to the cockpit itself, the most noticeable of which was the installation of a multifunction display. Other changes affected the undercarriage and stub wings.

During the Afghanistan war the Soviets had discovered that it was completely insufficient to arm an attack helicopter with just a few unguided rocket pods. On most missions in Afghanistan the outer underwing pylons remained empty. The OKB Mil therefore came up with the idea of shortening the Mi-24's stub wings and limiting them to the wingtip pylons. This change did not lead to a reduction in the helicopter's antitank capabilities, since all of the Mi-

Mi-24PN Specifications

Measurements	
Rotor diameter	56.75 ft.
Fuselage length	57.4 ft.
Overall length	65 ft.
Wingspan	21.5 ft.
Height	14.6 ft.
Rotor circular area	2,530 sq. ft.
Number of rotor blades	five-blade main rotor / three-blade tail rotor
Weights	
Empty weight	18,408 lbs.
Takeoff weight	24,030 lbs.
Maximum takeoff weight	26,015 lbs.
Fuel capacity	561 gal. + four 112 gal. auxiliary tanks
Power Plants	two TV3-117VMA turboshafts
Takeoff power	2 × 2,367 hp
Performance	
Maximum speed	195 mph at 3,280 ft.
Cruise speed	162 mph
Range	285 to 621 mi.
Hover to altitude	9,842 ft.
Ceiling	18,045 ft.
Rate of climb	up to 41 ft./sec.
Armament	
Revolving turret	one GSh-30-2K with 250 rounds
Weapons stations	four UB-32, each with thirty-two 57 mm rockets four B-8, each with twenty 80 mm rockets four bombs or cluster bombs two cannon pods eight Shturm-V or Ataka-V guided antitank missiles
Payload	5,291 lbs. eight passengers
Crew	two or three

Picture puzzle: one Mi-24PN in the midst of three Mi-24Ps. *Rostvertol PLC*

24PN's pylons were capable of carrying guided antitank missiles. The Mi-24V's quadruple launcher for guided antitank missiles had been tested successfully in 1986. This quadruple launcher could also be mounted on the Mi-24PN, so that the number of guided antitank missiles it carried remained the same as its predecessor,

The Mi-24PN's recognition feature was its "Buratino nose." Buratino is the name of the Russian version of the Pinocchio fairy tale. *Ablogin via Rostvertol PLC*

An Mi-24PN during takeoff. Note the pointed nose of the Saryevo night vision system, the shortened wings, and the fixed undercarriage. *Ablogin via Rostvertol*

The Mi-24PN was built in small numbers only. It was an interim type pending the introduction of the more modern Mi-35M. *Ablogin via Rostvertol*

the Mi-24P. The weapons system of the Mi-24PN had been so modernized that it could also use the modern Ataka-V guided antitank missile.

The reduction in size of the stub wings led to a weight savings, and the smaller wings also made the helicopter easier to fly in a hover, since the stub wings offered less resistance to the rotor downwash.

During the Afghanistan war it was found that the use of a tricycle undercarriage on helicopters could not be seen as the absolute best solution. While a retractable undercarriage reduced drag and thus enabled higher flying speed, tests showed that this advantage was only about 7 mph. The disadvantage of retractable undercarriages showed itself in emergency situations—the undercarriage had to be lowered before a forced landing. This took time, which was often not available because attack helicopters as a rule operated close to the ground. Ground contact often occurred before the undercarriage could be lowered. The damping characteristics of the undercarriage legs were thus ineffective. The Mi-24PN was therefore fitted with a fixed tricycle undercarriage,

which was lighter and more robust than the previous retractable undercarriage.

The sum of all these changes improved the combat value of the Mi-24PN quite considerably compared to the Mi-24P. Despite this, the Mi-24PN was built only in small numbers. It served as a transitional model to the much more capable Mi-24VK and Mi-35M.

The Mi-24PN saw action in Chechnya and in the conflict between South Ossetia and Georgia.

Mi-24PU1

The Mi-24PU1 was a local Ukrainian development of the Mi-24P. The main objective of this development was to replace Russian components with parts made in the Ukraine to the maximum extent possible.

The main difference between the Mi-24PU1 and the original Mi-24P was the installation of a modified engine: the TV3-M117VMA-SBM1V-02 engine, produced by the engine maker Motor Sich. There were also modifications in the cockpit, where a new GPS-supported navigation system and improved radio equipment were installed. A new laser target seeker was installed above the optical target acquisition system, directly above the cannon muzzle. The newly developed Adros KT-01AV self-defense system was also installed for protection against infrared-guided missiles.

Experience in the war in eastern Ukraine showed, however, that this system could not provide the helicopter with 100 percent protection against modern portable surface-to-air missiles (MANPADs). Nevertheless, Adros-KT combined with the AVU heat suppressors on the engine exhausts did prove extremely effective in low-altitude flight.

Mi-35M

The collapse of the Soviet Union represented a major turning point for the country's aviation industry. More or less overnight, the manufacturing and supplier factories were confronted with the situation of having to exist in several different states simultaneously. Longtime and proven cooperative arrangements were suddenly compromised or were no longer even possible. National egoism dominated.

The former main customer, the armed forces of the Soviet Union, did not exist any more. The Soviet Union's successor states all found themselves in a deep economic crisis and had no funds for costly armaments projects.

In the production centers at Arsenyev and Rostov on Don, the production lines were at a standstill. Highly qualified work forces had to be let go. It was an unimaginable condition for the men in the states that a short time ago had formed the mighty Soviet Union.

In Arsenyev the factory leadership decided henceforth to build only the Kamov helicopters favored by the new Russian leadership under Boris Yeltsin, and ordered the disassembly of the Mi-24 production line.

In contrast to this, in Rostov on Don they proceeded on the principle of hope and tried to keep the factory alive with repair contracts and minor modernization programs to Mi-24s already in service.

Russian Mi-35M.
Micheyev PLC

Recognition features of the Mi-35M are short wings and a fixed undercarriage. *Micheyev via Rostvertol PLC*

ВВС РОССИИ

RF-

ОПАСНО

50

Mi-35M Specifications

Measurements	
Rotor diameter	56.4 ft.
Fuselage length	57.4 ft.
Overall length	63 ft.
Wingspan	15.6 ft.
Height	13.6 ft.
Rotor circular area	2,500 sq. ft.
Number of rotor blades	five-blade main rotor / four-blade tail rotor
Weights	
Empty weight	18,417 lbs.
Takeoff weight	24,030 lbs.
Maximum takeoff weight	25,353 lbs. (ferry weight 26,455 lbs.)
Fuel capacity	561 gal. + four 112 gal. auxiliary tanks
Power Plants	two VK-2.500 turboshafts
Takeoff power	2 × 2,662 hp
Performance	
Maximum speed	192 mph
Cruise speed	162 mph
Range	285 to 621 mi.
Hover to altitude	10,170 ft.
Ceiling	18,864 ft.
Rate of climb	up to 41 ft./sec.
Armament	
Revolving turret	one GSh-23L with 450 rounds
Weapons stations	four UB-32, each with thirty-two 57 mm rockets four B-13, each with five 122 mm rockets four bombs or cluster bombs two cannon pods sixteen Shturm-V or Ataka-V guided antitank missiles
Payload	5,291 lbs. eight passengers
Crew	two or three

Other recognition features include new optics, the twin-barreled cannon in the revolving turret, and the X-shaped main rotor. *Micheyev via Rostvertol PLC*

These Mi-35Ms are carrying external fuel tanks. *Micheyev via Rostvertol PLC*

An Mi-35M escorting Mi-17 transport helicopters. *Micheyev via Rostvertol PLC*

Venezuelan
Mi-35M.
*Shaposhnikova
Rostvertol PLC*

Venezuela was the
first export
customer for the
Mi-25M.
*Shaposhnikova
Rostvertol PLC*

Shaposhnikova
Rostvertol PLC

Morales via
Rostvertol PLC

But there were also positive developments. At the beginning of the 1990s, microelectronics entered a rapid development phase. Suddenly, even the Russian helicopter manufacturers had access to computers with previously unimagined capabilities. Much that had previously been possible only in a dream was suddenly feasible. The know-how to make these dreams reality was available both in the Mil design bureau and in the manufacturing plant in Rostov on Don. Work began.

The first realization of these ideas, the Mi-24VM, was presented in 1995. It was based on the Mi-24VP, which had been built in small numbers. Modern computers made it possible to redesign the cockpit as a glass cockpit. Modern multifunction displays replaced the analog technology previously used with its round instruments. New optics for guidance of the guided antitank missiles were introduced, and armament options were supplemented by quadruple launchers for guided antitank missiles. To save weight, the retractable undercarriage was done away with and replaced by a fixed undercarriage, and the stub wings were shortened.

Designated Mi-35M, the helicopter was displayed at various aviation trade fairs, including the ILA in Berlin.

But at first, success didn't come. Although the militaries of various states showed interest in the Mi-35M, it found no buyers, since it was thought risky to purchase a product that the armed forces of the maker's country were not themselves prepared to introduce.

At the end of the 1990s, with the gradual improvement in the Russian economy, the picture changed. The Russian military, more or less healed from its temporary euphoria for the Kamov Ka-50, now also showed an interest in a modern variant of the tried-and-true Mi-24 and so provided the initial spark for further development.

Brazilian Mi-35M.
*Lucchesi via
Rostvertol PLC*

View from the cockpit of a Brazilian Mi-35M over the Amazon basin. *Lucchesi via Rostvertol PLC*

*Morales via
Rostvertol PLC*

In 2000, the leadership of Rostvertol, the manufacturing plant in Rostov on Don, at its own risk but with the support of the Mil helicopter plant in Moscow, decided to develop an improved variant of the Mi-35M. All the experience gained in recent years with the Mi-28N flowed into this version. A mockup was built and, that same year, was presented to the military.

In 2002, the Mi-35M prototype made its debut at the Paris Airshow at Le Bourget. Its abilities, which were clearly superior to all previous Mi-24 variants, aroused great interest among experts and military men from the countries that operated the Mi-24 in any capacity.

In 2003, Rostvertol received the green light from the Kremlin, and official flight trials began. During testing the Mi-35M displayed considerably improved maneuverability and rate of climb; nothing more stood in the way of service introduction. The Mi-35M was also approved for export.

The Mi-35M was initially offered as a modernization package in five different modules. Module 1 contained measures to extend the operating life of the helicopter airframe. Module 2 comprised the integration of the Mi-28 rotor system and more-powerful engines. Module 3 offered the conversion from a retractable to a fixed undercarriage. Module 4 concerned itself with the integration of the latest Russian weapons systems, such as the Ataka guided antitank missile, including launchers for eight missiles, and the Igla air-to-air missile, with a six-round launcher. Module 5 offered a modern cockpit and improved night combat capabilities.

The first customer for the Mi-35M was Venezuela, which began receiving its helicopters in 2006. Other customers followed. Interest in the Mi-35M was so great that Rostvertol stopped offering the

Forward view of the Mi-35M. *Micheyev via Rostvertol PLC*

Mi-35M only in the form of modernization packages and instead began building new helicopters in 2004. The Russian military also purchased the Mi-35M and introduced it into service. The designation Mi-24MV was not used. It can be assumed that this was done for marketing reasons and was intended to show that there was no longer any difference in performance between export machines and the attack helicopters built for Russian use.

Among the Russian units deployed to Syria in 2016 were those operating the Mi-35M. It was equipped with the latest sensors and more-capable systems for defense against infrared-guided missiles.

The Mi-35M has undergone a continual process of development and, together with the Mi-28N, will form the backbone of Russian frontal aviation in the near future.

Russia's equivalent to the US president's Marine One. *Chortos via Wiki*

Mi-24VK / Mi-24PK

The Mi-24VK was a development that was intended to further improve the night-fighting capability of the Mi-24. While it was planned to equip the Mi-24VK-1 with French components, the Mi-24VK-2 version used domestic components exclusively.

The Mi-24VK and its counterpart the Mi-24PK, based on the Mi-24P, were offered to the Russian military. But since the Mi-35M, which had a similar performance, was already entering frontline service, the Russian military rejected the Mi-24VP. It has also failed so far to achieve any export sales.

Mi-35MS

One of the most mysterious variants of the Mi-24 family is the Mi-35MS. It was first observed in 2013, when it completed flight trials at the Rostvertol manufacturing plant at Rostov on Don. Just three of these aircraft, whose operational purpose was not known for a long time, are thought to have been built. It is suspected that they are command-and-control helicopters for senior commanders, comparable to the Mi-9 of the 1980s. Other observers believe that the Mi-35MS is a highly specialized helicopter for

electronic warfare. Still others suspect that the Mi-35MS is intended to serve as the Russian president's personal helicopter and is thus the counterpart to the Marine One helicopter of the American president.

It was concluded that the Mi-35MS is a special version for the Russian president because of its special paint scheme. The machine is painted in an unusual shade of green, with the Russian flag on its tail. The observed registration numbers have always been of civilian origin, and military insignia have so far not been seen.

Larger windows than any other version of the Mi-24 also suggest that the Mi-35MS could be a VIP version.

In mid-2015, Russian media published photos of Russian president Vladimir Putin onboard an Mi-35MS. This proved that the Mi-35MS must be a special variant for the Russian president.

The Mi-35MS is largely based on the Mi-35M attack helicopter variant. It has the same shortened stub wings, a fixed undercarriage, and a main rotor system that originates from the Mi-28N.

One noticeable feature is the large aerodynamic fairing, whose shape is reminiscent of the radar noses of the Tu-95. Whether this fairing houses a radar system or communications equipment is not known.

Mi-24 Super Hind beside an AH-1 Rooivalk. *Bob Adams*

Indian Mi-35s were updated by Israeli companies. *Indian Air Force*

The purpose of the tubular containers at the ends of the stub wings is also a mystery.

It can be seen that the Mi-35MS is equipped with modern self-defense systems for defense against guided missiles.

Super Hind

The Republic of South Africa was subject to an international arms embargo for many years because of its apartheid policies. An independent and capable South African aviation industry therefore developed out of necessity. This industry developed the AH-2 Rooivalk attack helicopter to meet the requirements of the South African Army. It was tailored to the raw conditions of the bush war.

In the late 1990s, the ATE company began integrating some of the modern components developed for the Rooivalk into the Mi-24 in order to offer the resulting modernization package on the market.

The Mk. II modernization package integrated modern optics and observation equipment into the Mi-24P and its export variant, the Mi-35P. The Mk. III was tailored to the Mi-24V or Mi-35. Both these packages included integration of the South African ZT35 Ingwe and ZT-6 Mokopa guided antitank missiles into the weapons system, made the cockpit compatible with night vision goggles, and installed a modern computer. The optional dust filters for the engines were adapted directly from the Rooivalk.

The Mk. III replaced the 12.7 mm Yak-B machine gun with the M693 (F2) 20 mm cannon. This weapon had an ammunition capacity of 840 rounds.

A variant designated the Super Hind Mk. IV was sold to Algeria and Azerbaijan. In Azerbaijan the thus-modified machines were given the designation Mi-24G, the G being the abbreviation for the Azerbaijani word for night (*Geka*).

Interestingly, in recent years Azerbaijan has also procured the contemporaneous Russian model the Mi-35M, instead of modernizing more of its own Mi-24s to Mi-24G standard.

The most modern variant was the Super Hind Mk. V, which had a redesigned nose in which the pilot sat in the front cockpit and the gunner was housed in the rear cockpit. Distribution of the helicopter's armor was changed, so that the Super Hind Mk. V was about 3,968 pounds lighter than a comparable original Mi-24.

All South African Mi-24 modernization packages shared the ability to operate a broad spectrum both of South African and Russian weapons systems.

Israeli Hind Upgrades

The Israeli aviation industry was and is known for its ability to effectively modernize foreign aircraft. It all began with the Kfir, which was an Israeli development of the Mirage 5, progressed through the Kurnass 2000 based on the F-4E Phantom, and extends to the MiG-21, which was successfully offered from the 1990s onward. It is not surprising, therefore, that two Israeli companies brought to the market two competing modernization packages for the Mi-24. Israel Aerospace Industries (IAI) offered its package called Mission 24, which included a modernized night-vision-goggle-capable cockpit, modern optics, a helmet-mounted sight for the machine gun, GPS navigation, and

Mi-24 prototype with Fenestron tail rotor. *OKB Mil*

improved self-defense systems. It was sold to the Indian military, among others.

The Elbit company worked out a modernization package that significantly improved the helicopter's night-fighting capabilities and included a modern missile-warning system. Elbit also offered a cockpit modification that made it possible for the helicopter to fly with night vision goggles. Other options included NATO-compatible radio systems, a GPS-based navigation system, and a helmet-mounted sight for the helicopter's machine gun. Sri Lanka, Macedonia, and Georgia updated some of their Mi-24s with Elbit's help.

Unsuccessful Mi-24 Variants

The list of Mi-24 variants that did not enter production is a long one. Several of these are mentioned here.

During testing of the V-24, an attempt was made to use a shrouded rotor. Tail rotors of this kind are the trademark of French helicopters such as the Gazelle and today are often found on aircraft produced by the helicopter division of Airbus (formerly Eurocopter). The French term "Fenestron" has come to be accepted for tail rotors of this kind.

At least one V-24 prototype was fitted with a Fenestron tail rotor in 1975. Flight testing showed, however, that the tail rotor was not effective enough for a helicopter in the Mi-24's weight class, and consequently this line of development was abandoned.

Another unsuccessful variant was the Mi-24BMT (*isdeliye* 248). It is mentioned only in the literature, and the author is not aware of any photographs of this version. The BMT is believed to have been a version of the Mi-24B that was supposed to have been used with towed minesweeping equipment.

The Mi-24M (*isdeliye* 247) was developed for use by the navy. Since the navy traditionally selected helicopters made by Kamov, the Mi-24M got no further than the drawing board.

During the war in Afghanistan, the Soviet military realized that the enemy had developed a potentially successful tactic for combating Mi-24 attack helicopters. The *dushmani* remained under cover until the helicopters had overflown their positions, then opened fire from behind. To counter this tactic, an attempt was made to integrate a ventral gun position into the Mi-24. A narrow crawlway was created, leading to a glazed canopy in which a 12.7 mm NSVT Utyos machine gun was flexibly mounted. The flight engineer had to crawl to the position on his belly and also operate the weapon from the prone position. Testing showed the position to be impractical.

A tactical solution was ultimately found for the problem. Henceforth, Mi-24s operated in mixed formations with special Mi-17 transport helicopters. The rear door was removed from these Mi-17s, and an automatic weapon, either a Yak-B 12.7 or a GShG 7.62, was installed in its place. Tail gunners now covered the rear of the formation and suppressed any enemy activity with massed fire.

LL-PSV

The public first learned of the LL-PSV project (alias Mi-PSV, alias Mi X-1) during the MAKS airshow in Moscow in 2015. The new helicopter on display was reminiscent of an Mi-24 without stub wings, and its civilian finish gave rise to much speculation. It was conjectured that the Moscow helicopter maker Mil intended the machine to be a fast helicopter for wealthy private customers.

This was not so, however. The LL-PSV was conceived as a technology demonstrator, and the Moscow helicopter maker designated it a "flying laboratory for a future high-speed helicopter" (летающая лаборатория перспективного скоростного вертолета [ЛЛ ПСВ]).

The newly developed LL-PSV made its first flight on December 29, 2015. The crew for this maiden flight consisted of test pilot Vladimir Kutanin and test engineer Tatyana Demyanenko. After the flight, the crew praised the machine's excellent flight characteristics.

The main goal of the LL-PSV project, which was financed by the Russian state to the tune of 630 million rubles, was and is to research the basic scientific and technological principles for increasing the speed of helicopters by one and a half times that of current production machines.

The prototype LL-PSV was created from an Mi-24K battlefield reconnaissance helicopter whose nose section was completely redesigned. The previous TV3-117V engines were replaced by a newly developed variant with the designation VK-2500M.

The machine lacked stub wings during the demonstration at MAKS 2015, and also during its maiden flight. However, photos taken in spring 2016 show the LL-PSV again with stub wings, on whose pylons were mounted external fuel tanks.

A-10 World Record Helicopter

In 1975, the OKB Mil was given the task of capturing the world speed record for helicopters of the Soviet Union.

An earlier V-24 prototype still equipped with the short cockpit was chosen for this task, and it was converted into the Mi-24A-10 world record machine.

The first thing the developers had to do to achieve their assigned task was to reduce weight; therefore, all components that were not absolutely vital were removed. The armor, the armament and associated sensors, and even the stub wings were removed. It was also important to increase engine power, and so the aircraft's TV3-117 engines were replaced by more-powerful TV3-117s from the second series.

Thus prepared, on July 16, 1975, the Mi-24A-10 took to the air. Its crew consisted of two female pilots: in the pilot's seat was Galina Rastorguyeva, and at her side was Lyudmilla Polyanskaya. They achieved a maximum speed of 341.35 kilometers (km) per hour (212 mph) over a closed 15 / 25 km (9.3 / 15.5 mile) circuit. On June 18, 1975, they established another women's world record by reaching an average speed of 336.464 km (209 miles) per hour on a 100 km (62-mile) circuit.

On August 1, Lyudmilla Polyanskaya flew the helicopter to a new women's world record over a distance of 500 km (310 miles), achieving an average speed of 331.023 km (205 miles) per hour.

On August 8, 1975, the helicopter set a new climb record. Galina Rastorguyeva reached the 3,000-meter (9,842-foot) mark in 2 minutes, 33.5 seconds.

On August 13, the female pilots covered the 1,000 km (620-mile) distance with an average speed of 333 km (206 miles) per hour and, on August 26, succeeded

ABOVE: *Russkiye Vertolyoty*

RIGHT: *MinProm-Torg Rossiy*

In the initial phase of flight testing, the prototype is intended to reach a maximum speed of 250 mph. In a second phase an attempt will be made to further increase maximum speed to 280 mph and even higher.

While the LL-PSV is based on the Mi-24 attack helicopter, it also differs from it considerably. The airframe has been redesigned to minimize drag and improve flight behavior at high speeds.

The main rotor was completely redesigned. It received innovative rotor blades made of composite materials that were developed at Mil in Moscow and built in a pilot program. The rotor blades exhibit improved aerodynamic characteristics and were shaped on the basis of the latest discoveries in the field of aerodynamics.

During flight trials the developer hoped to obtain data confirming models worked out in a wind tunnel. Should the LL-PSV project prove to be successful, the knowledge gained could be used in the further development of helicopter types already in service.

in climbing to 6,000 m (19,680 feet) in seven minutes and forty-three seconds.

For reasons of secrecy, the Mi-24A-10 was entered as the A-10 only in the record documents of the International Aeronautical Federation. For the same reasons, the female pilots were photographed in the cockpit of an Mi-8.

To break the absolute speed record for helicopters, several changes to the main rotor and engine were necessary. Three years later, on September 21, 1978, Mil test pilot Gurgen Karapetyan established an absolute speed record for helicopters with a top speed of 368.4 km (228.9 miles) per hour.

This record held until 1986, when it was broken by a modified Westland Lynx.

The Path to the Successor Model

Mikhail Leontyevich Mil had proposed a hypothesis that in developing a fully capable attack helicopter, which would essentially be the flying counterpart of the modern standard tank, it would be more favorable to proceed in stages. One should first develop a technologically less complex "flying machine" and then develop the "flying tank."

A look into the situation in the United States, where the attempt to create a technologically advanced attack helicopter, the AH-56A Cheyenne, was a grandiose failure, proved the correctness of this theory. Because of this failure, for a long time the US had to get by with the AH-1 Cobra, an interim solution that ultimately proved to be not bad in service, but that could not justify the American claim to be the leading technological power in the world.

In the Soviet Union, Mil created the Mi-24 "flying armored personnel carrier" and successfully took the first step toward the "flying tank."

In 1968, when work on the Mi-24 prototypes *isdeliye* 240 had just begun, Mikhail L. Mil began giving thought to the shape of the "flying tank." He set down his ideas in several sketches and gave the project its designation V-28 or Mi-28.

His sketches were not expanded into a full project, since the OKB more than had its hands full with other projects. As well, Mil was suffering from a stress-related illness from which he would never completely recover.

OKB Mil

OKB Mil

Not until three years after Mil's death was the "flying tank" project revived. This time it was pushed ahead under the leadership of Marat Tishchenko. In 1973, with the Mi-24 entering service and the creation of the Mi-24D, neither the military nor the OKB knew precisely what a "flying tank" would look like. They therefore oriented themselves toward American developments, where the AAFSS program had been canceled and the Advanced Attack Helicopter (AAH) project was coming alive.

Building on this, requirements were specified for the Mi-28. It was supposed to be faster than the Mi-24. Maximum speed had to be between 236 and 260 mph. All-weather capability was demanded, as was night-fighting capabilities. Armor thicknesses were to be such that the helicopter could withstand armor-

piercing 12.7 mm bullets and 20 mm high-explosive fragmentation shells. Armament was to be at least eight Shturm guided antitank missiles, and a flexibly mounted 30 mm cannon and weapons load could not be less than 2,645 pounds.

Great emphasis was placed on crew survivability, and thus the installation of ejection seats was envisaged.

The Mi-28 was supposed to be a fast attack helicopter providing air support to ground forces and following the tactics of the earlier close-support aircraft. In addition the Mi-28 was to provide escort for transport helicopters and engage enemy helicopters in aerial combat, and all this with a maximum weight limit of 25,353 pounds.

The OKB chose two fundamentally different approaches. The first was based on the Mi-24 with the freight compartment removed, resulting in a much more slender fuselage. Instead of being arranged side by side in pairs, the engines were separated and attached to the fuselage sides. The stub wings were in a low-wing arrangement and had just four pylons; however, these could be fitted with quadruple launchers for guided antitank missiles. This project abandoned the Mi-24's tricycle undercarriage, and the Mi-28 was given a tailwheel undercarriage. The main undercarriage was retractable, while the tailwheel was not.

The cockpit arrangement was strongly reminiscent of the Mi-24. The pilot again sat in the rear, while the gunner occupied the forward cockpit.

The second approach looked completely futuristic. It painted a picture of the Mi-28 that differed dramatically from all other helicopters in the world.

In this design, only the nose section was remotely reminiscent of the Mi-24. Here, too, there were separate cockpits for the pilot and gunner; the external shape of this cockpit was reminiscent of the Mi-24. The nose section merged into a long, slender fuselage that ended in a cruciform tail reminiscent of the World War II–era Dornier Do 335. Like the Do 335, it had a pusher propeller.

Just behind the nose section on the slender fuselage were the wings. These were real wings, not stub wings, which were attached to the fuselage in a shoulder wing arrangement. Mounted at the end of each wing was a transmission, above which was a rotor with a diameter of 33.8 feet. The engine was positioned beneath the transmission.

From the transmission shafts led to a central transmission in the fuselage, which by means of a shaft drove the tail propeller and established a connection to the rotor transmission in the other wing. Thus the Mi-28 was supposed to remain flyable even after the loss of an engine.

Mi-28N with an Mi-35M in the background. *Anna Parchomenko via Rostvertol PLC*

The Mi-28N firing its cannon. *Soldatkin via Rostvertol PLC*

Anna
Parchomenko
Rostvertol PLC

There were three pylons beneath each wing to carry weapons or fuel tanks. The main undercarriage retracted rearward into the wings, and the tailwheel was fixed.

Mockups were built of the two Mi-28 variants. The first version was ultimately selected, since Hughes had entered the similarly configured Model 77 in the AAH competition in the US.

The preliminary final design of the Mi-28 was decided on in 1976, and on December 16, 1976, the Central Committee of the Communist Party and the Council of Ministers of the Soviet Union issued a development contract.

On the dame day, the OKB Kamov was given permission to develop its V-80 project to prototype status. In the course of time, the rival V-80 model would become the Ka-50 attack helicopter.

At OKB Mil, work on the Mi-28 now began in earnest. By the end of 1977, it had largely agreed with the subcontractors about the size and performance of the components to be delivered. Work on the final design, which differed from the mockup in several respects, began in 1979.

Construction of the first two prototypes began in August 1980 without waiting for official approval of the final mockup by the party and the military. Not until 1981 did they give the green light, by which time the first prototype was half completed and the airframe for structural trials was already being tested.

The first prototype was completed in July 1982. On November 10 of the same year, the Mi-28 flew for the first time, and on December 19, the first flight over a longer distance was carried out. State trials began on December 20 and continued until 1984. They progressed so satisfactorily that the Minister for Aircraft Construction ordered the helicopter factory in Arsenyev to switch to production of the Mi-28. Series production was supposed to begin in 1987.

By then, several improvements had become necessary that had to be implemented before the Mi-28A, the first production version. In 1986, the Mi-28 achieved all the required performance parameters and even exceeded several of the requirements. Nothing should have stood in the way of quantity production.

There was opposition within the military, however. A powerful Kamov lobby worked to promote the futuristic Ka-50 and was successful. In 1984, the defense ministry opposed the Ministry for Aircraft Construction and ordered the Arsenyev factory to switch production to the Ka-50. The Rostov on Don factory subsequently began establishing an Mi-28 production line.

Head-to-head flight trials between the Mi-28 and Ka-50 took place in April 1986; the Mi-28 won in every performance category. Despite this, the leading military men still insisted on the Ka-50.

Production of the Mi-28A began at Rostov on Don in 1987. In 1988, the helicopter was shown to the world at the Paris Airshow. The aviation experts were impressed.

The confusion of perestroika and glasnost and the subsequent collapse of the Soviet Union prevented plans for mass production from being realized. The state was out of money. The helicopter manufacturer at Rostov on Don found itself in a critical situation.

In 1993, the Mi-28A was shelved. Comparisons with Western helicopters had shown that the Mi-28A had some catching up to do with respect to night-fighting capabilities and aircraft electronics. The result was the Mi-28N.

The first prototype of the Mi-28N was built in 1996. It made its maiden flight in November of the same year. State flight trials began in April 1997, including a live-fire trial during the second Chechen War. Here, too, the two-seat Mi-28 showed itself to be clearly superior to the single-seat Ka-50. Testing went on into 2002. Then the commander of the air forces of the Russian Federation declared that the Mi-28N would be the future standard helicopter. In 2003, this statement was confirmed by Russian president Putin at the MAKS air display in Moscow. The first preproduction helicopter took to the air for the first time in March 2004. Official production began in 2006, followed by entry into service with the Russian military.

The Mi-28NE version was produced for export. In 2016, this variant received its baptism of fire in the hands of Iraqi pilots battling radical Islamic rebels in the Sunni Triangle of Iraq.

Many components developed for the Mi-28, Mi-28A, and Mi-28N were adopted for the Mi-24 family over time. These included the main rotor and X-shaped tail rotor, optical equipment, more-powerful engines, and weapons systems originally developed for the Mi-28.

Code Names and Nicknames

Over the years the Mi-24 was given many other names in addition to the official type designations. Some of them will be related here.

When the project for an attack helicopter became ripe for decision, Mikhail Leontyevich Mil called it LBMP, or *Letayushchaya Boyevaya Maschina Pechota* (летающая боевая машина пехота), which roughly translated means "flying combat machine of the infantry."

He sometimes also used the designation VBMP as an abbreviation of *Vertolyotnaya Boyevaya Maschina Pechota* (вертолётная боевая машина пехота), or "helicopter combat machine of the infantry."

The LBMP and VBMP soon became the V-24, with the *V* standing for *Vertolyot* or helicopter.

Internally the V-24 was always called the Mi-24. "Mi" was the abbreviation for the Mil experimental design bureau, or OKB Mil for short. The OKB Mil was and is often viewed in the West as the producer of the Mi-24, but that is not entirely true. In the Soviet

Mi-24A, nickname Veranda, serving with the Group of Soviet Forces in Germany. *Alexander Pushkarev via www.16va_be*

Mi-24V, nickname "Crocodile." *MLM via www.16va_be*

The Mi-24 was called *sheitan arba* by the enemy in Afghanistan. To the Russian forces it was "Crocodile" or "Angel of the Skies." *US DoD*

Union, aircraft design bureaus and the factories that built the aircraft were organizationally separated. While there were personal interrelationships between the OKB and the manufacturer, resulting from many years of cooperation, ultimately the two sides were independent of one another.

In Soviet military service the Mi-24 was initially called *dvazat-chet-verok*, which can be translated as "twenty-four." The initial service version, the Mi-24A, was also called the veranda. This nickname was based on the extensive cockpit glazing, which had the unpleasant habit of heating the cockpit like a greenhouse in strong sunlight.

The attack helicopter earned its ultimate nickname when the Mi-24D arrived on the scene: the units called it "Crocodile." When some imagination was used by the observer, the Mi-24D's nose, as viewed from the side, bore a certain resemblance to the head of a crocodile. The helicopter's standard green camouflage was also reminiscent of that predatory reptile.

To the fighting troops in Afghanistan, the Mi-24 helicopters were "Angels of the Air," or sometimes also "Archangel" or "Avenging Angel."

The Afghan rebels hated the Mi-24 like the plague and had a terrible fear of the attack helicopter. They gave it the name *sheitan arba*, which means "devil's war wagon" or "devil's chariot."

In the East German land forces, the Mi-24 attack helicopters were sometimes called "Dragons" or "Hussars." These nicknames, which were not very widespread, probably went back to the attack helicopter wing's honorary names Adolf von Lützow and Ferdinand von Schill. The designation Mi-24 was used in the vernacular, or "the 24" for short. It was always "die 24" (feminine) and never "der 24" (masculine). In keeping with an old tradition, the Mi-24 attack helicopter's designation was feminine. This was true of all other aircraft and helicopters in the German Democratic Republic.

In Venezuela the Mi-35M was given the name "Caribe"; the Caribe were a warlike Indian tribe from the pre-Columbian time. The name is official and appears on the noses of the helicopters.

In Cyprus the National Guard's Mi-35Ps are called "black panthers" because of their night-black finish.

NATO assigned every Soviet aircraft a code name. The first letter of the name indicated the aircraft's purpose. If it began with a *B*, then the aircraft was a bomber, if it began with an *F* then the aircraft was a fighter or fighter-bomber, if it began with a *C* it was a transport, and if it began with an *H* it was a helicopter.

Mi-24D in service with the NVA, nickname "Hussar," "Dragoon," or "the 24." *Rob Schleiffert*

A Venezuelan Caribe. *Sergio J. Padrón A. via Rostvertol*

Cypriot Black Panther. *Rostvertol PLC*

The Mi-24 was given the code name "Hind," which, like all code names, is of English origin.

To distinguish between individual versions of an aircraft or helicopter, a capital letter was added to the name, separated by a dash. This did not take place in the sequence in which the machines were developed in the Soviet Union, but rather as the West got wind of their existence. In NATO jargon the Mi-24A was designated Hind A. Logically, the Mi-24B should have received the code name Hind B; however, Western intelligence remained unaware of the existence of this version of the attack helicopter for a long time. Instead, the intelligence experts discovered variants of the Mi-24 with a short cockpit, straight wings, and launch rails for guided antitank missiles beneath the wings. The West thought that this was a new version of the Mi-24 and gave it the code name Hind B. Not until much later did NATO recognize that the helicopters it had designated Hind B had actually been prototypes and preproduction aircraft.

The Mi-24U trainer was correctly identified as a new version and henceforth designated Hind C. The Mi-24D became the Hind D; the Mi-24V, the Hind E; and the Mi-24P, the Hind F. The Mi-24RKhR chemical reconnaissance version was inexplicably named Hind G1, and the Mi-24K battlefield reconnaissance helicopter, the Hind G2.

The last version of the Mi-24 built in the Soviet Union, the Mi-24VP, received the code name Hind H.

In the beginning, during the early years of the Cold War, for reasons of secrecy the Soviet Union was reluctant to release the official type designations for highly developed military technology. Oftentimes even the code names given to weapons systems were absolutely secret, which led to media reporters having to describe the technology. These descriptions often revealed more about a weapons system than publishing the type designation or code name could ever have done. Since it did not know the Soviet type designations, NATO adopted the above-described system of code names.

Later, when the Soviet Union no longer kept its type designations secret, NATO nevertheless retained its system of code names. And so it remains to the present day. Now, however, it is more difficult to learn the NATO code names than it is the official type designations of Russian or Chinese aircraft.

Therefore the NATO code names for the modern representatives of the Mi-24 family, such as the Mi-24PN and the Mi-35M, are unknown.

This Mi-24D is on
display at the
airfield museum in
Cottbus. *Normann*

The Mi-24 in Detail

The Mi-24 was a twin-engined, armored helicopter with stub wings, retractable undercarriage, a five-blade main rotor, and a three- or four-blade tail rotor.

The Mi-24's crew consisted of two men, a pilot and gunner, with the pilot seated in the rear cockpit and the gunner in front.

In unit service it proved advantageous to add a third man to the crew. The third crew member's position was on a sort of stool in the very narrow passageway to the cargo space, and he operated as flight engineer, gunner, or both from the cargo compartment.

The Mi-24 was of all-metal, monocoque construction. The airframe nose section covered frames 1N to 6N. It housed the crew, the cockpit equipment, the aircraft's machine gun and ammunition, and the guidance and control technology for the guided antitank missiles. In the Mi-24A, Mi-24B, and Mi-24U versions, the crew was accommodated in a single generously dimensioned cabin, which was heavily glazed and spacious. Astonishingly, however, the view provided the crew was not optimal, since the glazing's extensive framing limited the field of view and produced reflections that further restricted the view. The pilot and gunner sat slightly offset to provide a better forward view. Nevertheless, the gunner partially blocked the pilot's forward view, and the blind spot caused by the offset seating arrangement was unusually large. Beginning with the Mi-24D, therefore, a two-part cockpit was used that was staggered vertically and provided an optimal view for both crew members. To improve the view to the rear, large rearview mirrors were retrofitted to the exterior.

Armor glass panels protected the crew against small-arms fire from in front. The thickness of the armor glass panels was such that they could withstand 12.7 mm armor-piercing rounds. The armor glass panels could be heated, and there was a standard automobile windshield wiper to remove rainwater.

The cockpit side glazing was Plexiglas and therefore not bulletproof. Attempts to install additional armor glass panels inside the cockpit proved impractical and were therefore abandoned.

CHAPTER 3

The crew was protected by 0.3-inch armor plates incorporated into the external skin on the sides of the cockpit. The rounded, bullet-deflecting shape of the Mi-24's nose increased the effectiveness of its armor protection. To further protect the crew, the sides of the cockpit seats were designed to be solid and massive and bullet resistant. During combat sorties in Afghanistan, the crews also wore armored vests and helmets.

Access to the gunner's cabin was by way of the cockpit canopy, which opened upward on the left side. Two footsteps with automatic covers provided the gunner quick and safe entry. On the cockpit frame there was a massive leather handgrip, which served as an aid for entry and exit by the gunner.

The forward cockpit was characterized by the KPS-53AV (КПС-53АВ) machine gun control and targeting device located in the gunner's direct field of view. It was operated with both hands and was capable of moving the aircraft's machine gun in the vertical and horizontal planes. A target indication was projected onto the ASP-17V reflector sight, which always pointed in the same direction as the barrel. This solution was not perfectly ideal, since the gunner,

The external mirror enables the crewman to see the otherwise unobservable aft part of the helicopter. *Normann*

Cockpit section of the Mi-24D, with entrances to both cockpits open. *Normann*

Windshield wiper improves the view in rain. *Normann*

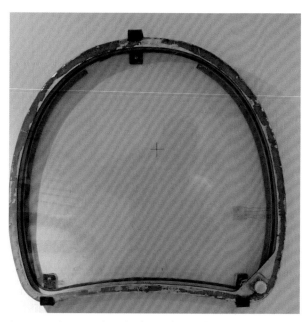

An armor-glass panel on display in the Cottbus airfield museum. *Normann*

Observation and control devices for guided antitank missiles; unfortunately, the sight is not present. *Normann*

Optics. *Artemenko via Mambour*

sitting strapped into his seat and wearing a helmet, had insufficient space to be able to exploit the weapon's entire range of movement. When firing to the side, his only option was to "fire from the hip," combined with the attempt to direct his fire onto the target by using tracer. A helmet-mounted sight was not introduced until updated new-build variants of the Mi-24 became available in 2004.

On the right side were the observation and control devices for use of the guided antitank missiles, as well as retrofitted controls for the flare dispensers. In the forward right side of the cockpit were the control elements for the use of bombs. Bombs could be dropped singly, in pairs, or all together. Jettisoning of the bombs was also possible.

The forward cockpit was equipped with a simple set of flight instruments and had a stick, a collective lever, and small foot pedals.

With the help of these control elements, the gunner could take control of the helicopter in an emergency. The forward cockpit could be hermetically sealed and was climate controlled. Comfortable to bearable conditions could be maintained in the cockpit within an external temperature range of −58 to +98.6 degrees Fahrenheit. For better mixing of the air in the cockpit, there was a small propeller with rubber blades. For flights at altitudes higher than 9,842 feet, the Mi-24 was equipped with an oxygen system with masks for the crew.

The pilot entered his cockpit by way of a massive door on the starboard side, which opened to the rear. Here again, automatically closing footsteps eased access to the cockpit. The Mi-24P had a metal

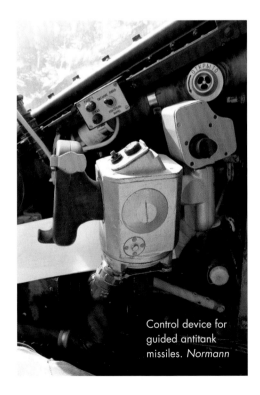

Control device for guided antitank missiles. *Normann*

Directly in the gunner's field of view is the KPS-35AV control and aiming device for the helicopter's machine gun.

Bomb-dropping panel. *Normann*

Visible in the lower right corner is the control box for the flare dispensers. *Normann*

Close-up of the gunner's control stick. *Normann*

strip beneath the door, which was supposed to block flames coming from the cannon breech.

The pilot's cockpit was equipped with a full set of flight and navigation equipment, which filled the entire space in front of the pilot. The instrumentation consisted of round instruments. Digital multifunction displays were not added until modern and updated cockpits were introduced.

In the pilot's field of view there was a PKV reflector gunsight. The pilot used this sight to aim unguided

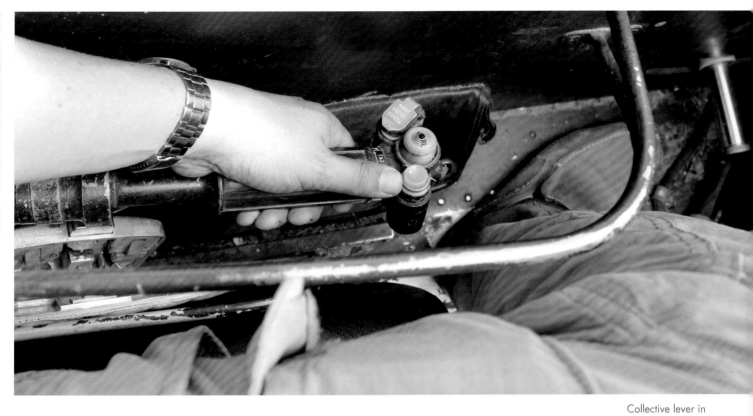

Collective lever in the gunner's cockpit. *Normann*

The gunner's stick. *Normann*

The foot pedals in the gunner's cockpit were very small in size. *Normann*

rockets and cannon pods, as well as the integral cannon of the Mi-24P. The PKV sight could also be used as a targeting aid for the flexibly mounted Yak-B machine gun; however, for this the gun had to be locked in the neutral position.

A HUD (Head-Up Display) was not introduced until it was retrofitted to updated Mi-24s. It is now standard on the latest variants, such as the Mi-35M.

Much of the radio equipment (VHF and short wave) was installed in the pilot's cockpit, as were all the indicators for the navigation system, which included the ARK-15M and ARK-2U radio compasses. Immediately visible was the large indicator panel, on which a cross icon (indicating the helicopter's actual position) could be displayed on a flight map. This indicator panel was linked to the Doppler navigation system. In modern versions of the Mi-24 this indicator panel has been replaced by color multifunction displays.

Door to the pilot's cockpit. *Normann*

The Mi-24D's instrument panel. *Normann*

The fan with rubber blades is a typical feature of Soviet cockpits. *Normann*

Cockpit section of a Cyprian Mi-35M. The rail under the cockpit door is clearly visible. *Rostvertol PLC*

Modern cockpit in
a Cyprian Mi-35P.
Rostvertol PLC

View from the cockpit of an Mi-24D. The PKV reflector gunsight can be seen in the center. *Normann*

Another variant of a modern Mi-35M cockpit. *Rostvertol PLC*

Modern cockpit in a Venezuelan Mi-35M. *Rostvertol PLC*

Head-up display (HUD) in an Mi-35P. Above the HUD is the indicator of the SPO-15 radar-warning device. *Rostvertol*

View looking half left. *Normann*

The SPU-8 intercom system was used for communication between crew members. Also present in the cockpit was the RI-65 voice information system, which warned the crew of threats as well as the exceedance or undershooting of flight parameters, such as exceeding maximum allowable airspeed, dangerous proximity to the ground, excessive angle

The controls arranged to the pilot's left. *Normann*

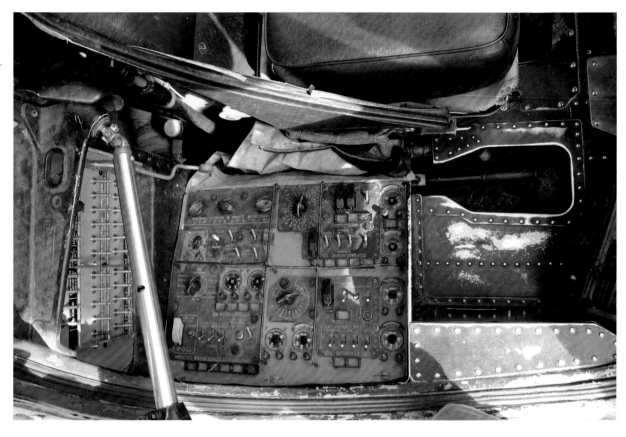

Controls to the pilot's right, located directly in the entrance area. *Normann*

Instruments and controls to the right of the instrument pane. *Normann*

of attack, etc. The warnings were delivered by a woman's voice, which could be very demanding. In Soviet helicopters the voice was that of a then very popular female telecaster who answered to the lovely first name of Natasha. In pilot's jargon, therefore, the voice information system was called "Natasha" or "nagging Nadia." Similar systems were also present in the MiG-29 and Su-27.

The weapons system also included IFF (identification friend or foe) and the radar-warning device. The SPO-10 was installed in early models, which provided a simple indication of the threat situation. The more modern SPO-15 was used in versions beginning with the Mi-24V, which enabled a much more precise assessment and analysis of incoming radar beams.

The Mi-24 was equipped with the SAU-V24-1 automatic helicopter control system. The VUAP-1 autopilot, which was part of the system, automatically maintained altitude and speed as well as automatic flight in a hover.

The control elements for the use of unguided rockets were located in the pilot's cockpit. With the help of the PUS-32 rocket-firing device, the pilot could

THE MI-24 IN DETAIL

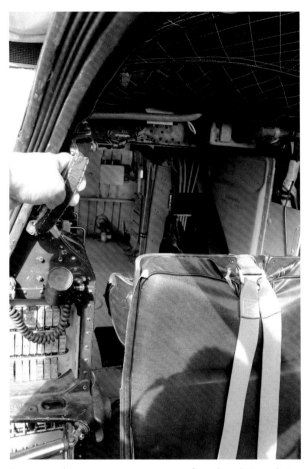

Passage to the cargo compartment seen from the pilot's cockpit.
Normann

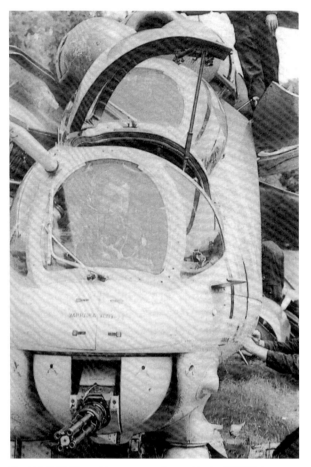

The Yak-B-12.7 machine gun was housed in the USPU-24
revolving turret. *US DoD*

select salvo sizes of 4, 8, 16, 32, and 64. In an emergency the pilot could jettison the rocket pods and guided antitank missile launch rails. As with the Mi-24D version, the pilot was also able to drop the bombs.

The pilot's cabin was connected to the freight compartment. Consequently it could be hermetically sealed only in conjunction with the freight compartment. It was air-conditioned and included a fan with rubber blades, typical of Soviet aircraft.

The Mi-24's machine gun or cannon armament was also installed in the fuselage nose. In the Mi-24A version it was right in the nose, whereas in the Mi-24D, Mi-24V, Mi-24VP, and Mi-35M the armament was housed in a revolving turret under the nose. The USPU-24 revolving turret was attached to frame 1N and enabled the weapon to be moved horizontally between −60 and +60 degrees and vertically from +20 to −40 degrees.

On the Mi-24P and following versions, the cannon was in a fixed mounting on the right side of the fuselage, beneath the cockpit glazing.

Ammunition was stored in the cockpit of the Mi-24A. In all other versions it was contained in a magazine beneath the pilot's cockpit.

Under the nose, beside the machine gun turret on the right (as seen in the direction of flight), was the gyrostabilized targeting and observation system for the guided antitank missiles. Protective caps prevented the optics inside from being damaged. The caps had to be opened to search for targets and employ the weapons.

To the left of the revolving turret, beneath an aerodynamic fairing, was the swiveling antenna for radio guidance of the guided antitank missiles.

Various measuring instruments were housed on the nose of the helicopter. These included the pitot

The Mi-24P's externally mounted cannon seen from the front. *Normann*

Mounting of the GSh-30-2K cannon seen from behind. *Rostvertol PLC*

tube for determining airspeed, the angle-of-attack sensor (attached to a mast), and the antennas for the radar-warning receiver and the SAU-24-1 close-range navigation system.

Under the nose was the semiretractable nosewheel undercarriage. The nosewheel leg had a hydropneumatic shock absorber, was steerable, and had twin wheels.

Tires measuring 480 × 280 mm (18.9 × 11 inches) were used. The nosewheel leg was attached to frame 4N and retracted rearward; the nosewheel leg on the Mi-24A and Mi-24U versions was slightly shorter. The Mi-24PN and Mi-35M had a nonretractable nosewheel.

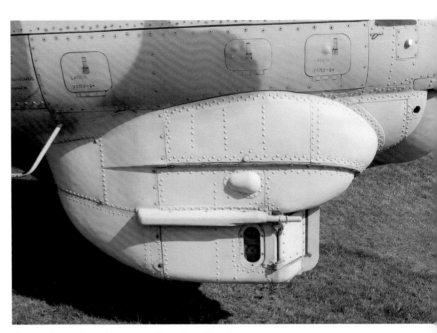

The missile-tracking device seen from the side. *Normann*

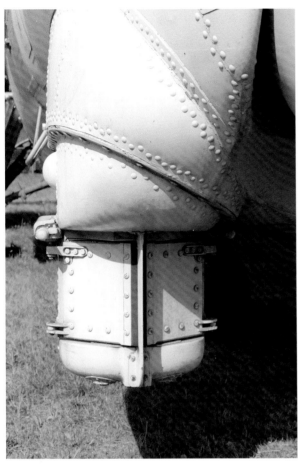

The Raduga complex's tracking equipment seen from the front. The protective doors are shut. *Normann*

The main undercarriage was designed to be completely retractable. It retracted into the aft part of the fuselage, turning 90 degrees. Exceptions were the Mi-24PN and Mi-35M, which had a fixed undercarriage. The wheel wells were closed by very large doors. The main undercarriage was also equipped with hydropneumatic shock absorbers.

While the nosewheel was unbraked, the main undercarriage wheels had independent brakes. On the ground the helicopter was steered using differential braking. The main undercarriage had 720×320 mm (28×12.6 inch) tires.

The undercarriage wheelbase was 14.4 feet; the track width, 9.9 feet.

Aft of the fuselage nose, which extended from frames 1N to 4N, was the center section of the helicopter airframe, with frames 1 to 15. It housed the cargo compartment, fuel tanks, engines, main transmission, and much more.

The Mi-24D had green covers, but from the Mi-24V onward, these were black. *Normann*

The main undercarriage. *Normann*

The Mi-24D's nosewheel retracted rearward. *Normann*

Tire size information: 720 x 320 Model Se. *Normann*

The cargo compartment extended from frames 1 to 8. It was connected to the pilot's cockpit by a very narrow passageway. In this passageway was the flight engineer's station.

From the outside, the cargo compartment was reached by way of two large folding doors; these were split horizontally in the middle, with the upper part opening upward and the lowed part downward. On the inside of the lower door section was a rail, which made it easier to climb in.

The freight compartment had four square windows on each side, all of which could be opened. Beneath the windows were folding brackets for defensive weapons. The brackets not only were suitable for attaching the Kalashnikovs. They also limited the weapon's field of fire, preventing damage to the main rotor. Above the windows there were attachments for flexible hoses, whose adapters could be attached to a Kalashnikov assault rifle's shell ejector. Powder gases were also sucked through these lines and vented outside.

The cargo compartment was able to accommodate eight fully equipped troops. Depending on how the helicopter was equipped, there were either two low benches or canvas seats attached in the center of the cargo compartment. The seats were so arranged that four soldiers faced to starboard and four to port.

The seats could easily be removed. In the medevac helicopter configuration, two stretchers in the form of

Passageway to the pilot's cockpit as seen from the cargo compartment. The flight engineer's seat was located in this very narrow passage. *Normann*

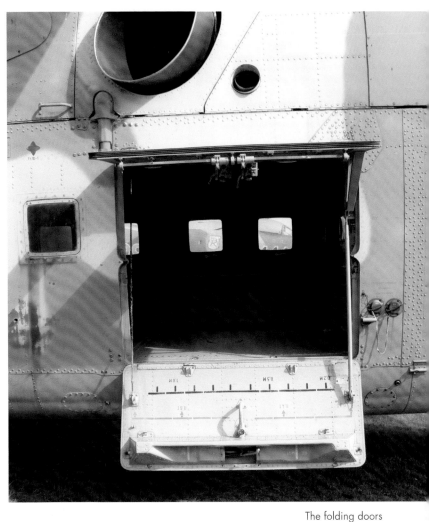

The folding doors were divided horizontally. *Normann*

A step on the lower door eased access to the cargo hold. *Normann*

The doors were bullet resistant and therefore quite thick. *Normann*

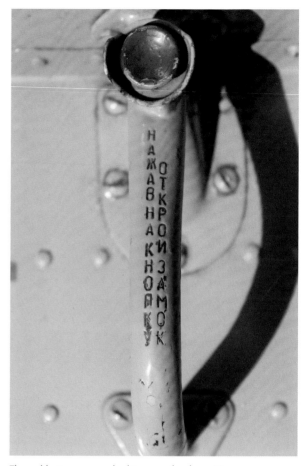

The red button was pushed to open the door. *Normann*

a bunk bed could be installed. There was also space for two seated wounded and a medic. It was also possible to configure the cargo compartment so that four prone wounded could be carried. In this configuration there was no room for a medical aide, however.

For medical purposes it was possible to install two additional oxygen bottles in the freight compartment.

Up to 3,300 pounds of freight could be carried in the cargo compartment. There were markings in the cargo compartment for precise placement of the cargo as well as tie-downs.

For ferry purposes, the cargo compartment of the Mi-24A to D versions could accommodate two

Cargo hold with bench seats. *Rostvertol PLC*

The cargo hold had square windows that could be opened.

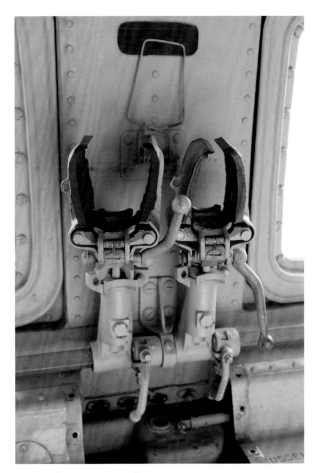

Brackets for mounting small arms. *Normann*

ABOVE: Small arms in position. *Rostvertol PLC*

LEFT: Polish Mi-24D in Afghanistan with a PK machine gun in the window. *US DoD*

Medevac version of the cargo hold. *Rostvertol*

fuel tanks with a capacity of 215 or 225 gallons each. Starting with the Mi-24V, this was no longer necessary since the modern versions were capable of carrying fuel tanks under the stub wings. Nevertheless, two fuel tanks could still be installed in the cargo compartment of the modern versions.

Unlike the versions mentioned above, the cargo compartment of the Mi-24RKhR chemical reconnaissance version was used to accommodate an analysis laboratory with work spaces for two mission specialists.

The cargo compartment of the Mi-24K battlefield reconnaissance version was used to accommodate a large aerial camera. This variant lacked the starboard entry door. In its place was a larger window through which the camera took its pictures.

Beneath the cargo compartment was a large fuel tank. It was made of flexible, textile-reinforced rubber with a layer of sealant. If the tank was pierced and the sealant came into contact with fuel, it immediately began to swell and in this way sealed the leak. Other fuel tanks were located behind the rear wall of the cargo compartment and behind the main transmission. They were also designed to be self-sealing. In total, 561 gallons were carried in five flexible tanks.

Loading instructions, which state that loads were to be placed so that their combined center of gravity was positioned between the blue and red pointers, which were marked with weights (in metric tons). The example states that a load with a total weight of 1 metric ton was supposed to be positioned between the pointers marked with "1T" and "1,5T." *Normann*

To improve survivability in combat and to prevent fire, the tanks can be filled with carbon dioxide. This task is carried out by the "neutral gas system." During flight, carbon dioxide is forced into the slowly emptying tanks, countering a potentially explosive mixture of fuel vapor and oxygen.

Above the cargo compartment are the two engines in a side-by-side arrangement, the auxiliary starter turbine and the main transmission.

Depending on the version, the helicopter is powered by different versions of the TV3-117. Each air-cooled turboshaft engine, weighing 628 pounds, has a twelve-stage axial compressor with variable-area guide vane. The first four stages of turbine blades are also automatically adjustable. The axial compressor is followed by an annular combustion chamber with twelve injection nozzles. The annular combustion chamber is followed by a second turbine, which by means of a shaft powers the axial compressor. Subordinate to it was a second turbine, which by means of a shaft leading to the main transmission delivered the actual output for propulsion. The two turbines are not interconnected; instead they are coupled together by gas dynamics.

Analysis station in the Mi-24RKhR. *Artemenko via Mambour*

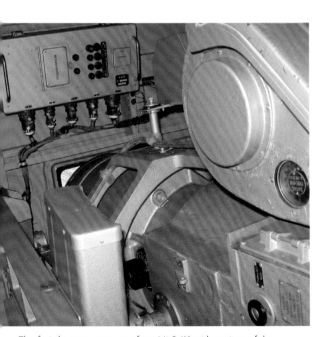

The freight compartment of an Mi-24K with a view of the AFA-100 reconnaissance camera. *Artemenko via Mambour*

After passing through the turbines, the exhaust gases are vented outside. Since hot exhausts provide an ideal target for infrared-guided missiles, as of 1984 the engine exhausts were modified so that a system to suppress and cool the exhaust gases could be mounted. Called AVU, the system consisted of two large boxes in which the hot exhaust gases were mixed with cooler surrounding air and then released into the rotor stream of the main rotor and swirled.

Fire-warning sensors are positioned in the area of the engines, which could activate a fire-extinguishing system should a fire break out. The extinguishing agent was kept in pressure bottles housed near the main undercarriage.

Because the TV3-117 series of engines were not self-starting, an AI-9V auxiliary turbine was located above the engines. It acted as starter for the TV3-117 engines.

Like all modern Mil helicopters, the Mi-24's engine cover panels were designed to double as work platforms. They could be opened to the side and provided unhindered access to the engines. They were so massive that they could easily support mechanics.

Armored elements 0.3 inches thick were incorporated into the engine covers, providing a high degree of survivability in the case of small-arms fire. The dust covers in front of the engine intakes are also armored.

The engines were followed by the main transmission, which delivers the torque produced by the engines in stages to the main rotor via a shaft to the tail rotor. It was so massively designed that it could operate for a certain time with just one engine running.

The Mi-24's main rotor was directly derived from the Mi-8's main rotor. It had five rotor blades that were equipped with flapping and drag hinges, as well as with drag dampers and automatically adjustable

The Mi-24's twin engines are mounted over the cargo compartment. Their air intakes are protected by dust covers. *Rostvertol PLC*

Shadow play: Afghan technicians working on an engine. *US Army, Cecilio M. Ricardo Jr.*

The rotor head of the Mi-24's main rotor. *Normann*

blade-flapping limiters. As seen from above, the rotor rotates clockwise, which is opposite to the direction of rotation of Western helicopters.

The rotor blades can be deiced electrically. They are designed to withstand small-arms fire. Made of aluminum, the blades are made up of individual segments, each of which is filled with a honeycomb structure. Eighteen sections together form a rotor blade. To better reveal the formation of cracks in the rotor blades, the blade spars are filled with compressed air.

The main rotor was tilted 2.3 degrees to the right. This arrangement was supposed to enable a smoother flight and simpler aiming when firing unguided rockets and fixed weapons. The main rotor hub was equipped with a rotor brake, which was supposed to prevent the rotor from turning for a lengthy period in the event of shutdown or uncoupled engines.

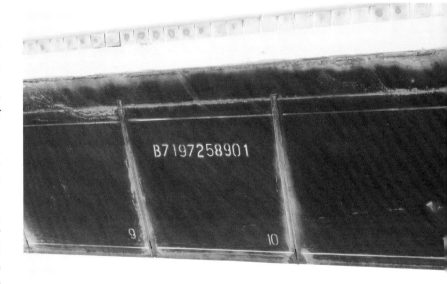

A segment of the main rotor. *Normann*

The Mi-35M introduced the newly developed main rotor of the Mi-28. The rotor head and hub are made of titanium, and the rotor blades are glass fiber composite materials. This makes the rotor lighter and more durable. It is supposed to remain flyable even after taking hits from 30 mm weapons.

There were stub wings mounted on both sides of the Mi-24's fuselage. On the one hand they served as auxiliary lift devices to unload the main rotor; on the other hand, they were used to carry weapons.

The stub wings were mounted on the aft part of the airframe, above the cargo compartment. It had 12 degrees of anhedral and an angle of attack of 19 degrees. The leading edge of the stub wings had 8.5 degrees of sweep. Depending on airspeed, the stub wings generated up to 25 percent of the total lift. This reduced loads on the main rotor, extended its life, and improved maneuverability. The stub wings consisted of a cantilever all-metal structure braced by nine spars.

There were two massive pylons beneath each wing; these could carry a total load of 3,300 pounds. The inner pylons were approved for a maximum of 1,100 pounds each, the outer pylons 550 pounds. They could be loaded with free-fall bombs, napalm canisters, cluster bombs, cannon pods, unguided rockets, and rocket pods. Starting with the Mi-24V version, the pylons were "wet," meaning they could carry fuel tanks. Each external fuel tank had a capacity of 112 to 118 US gallons.

Beginning with the Mi-24V version, the outer pylons could carry twin launchers for guided antitank missiles. Tests with quadruple launchers were carried out in the 1980s. Quadruple guided antitank missile launchers were standard equipment on the Mi-24PN and Mi-35M. Launchers

One of the main rotor blades. *Normann*

One of the Mi-24's stub wings as seen from the front.
Parchomenko Rostvertol PLC

Stub wing as seen from the side. *Normann*

for eight Ataka-V guided antitank missiles were also possible. A few Mi-24s operated by the Soviet military were equipped with launch rails for R-60M air-to-air missiles, but this configuration was not exported. Instead, the guided antitank missile launchers were modified so that they could use Igla man-portable surface-to-air missiles. With the Mi-35M there also appeared a launcher for six Igla missiles.

There was a gun camera on the port stub wing. On older versions it was placed on a pylon, but from the Mi-24D onward it was mounted above the end pylon. It disappeared from later Mi-24s.

To improve directional stability, the wingtips of the stub wings were canted downward. The jettisonable double racks for guided antitank missiles were mounted on these end pylons.

The gun camera as seen from the pilot's cockpit. *Normann*

The stub wing of an Mi-24A with UB-32 rocket pods and Falanga guided antitank missiles. The gun camera was placed over the inner pylon.

On the Mi-24RKhR the guided antitank missile launchers were replaced by shovellike digging systems for collecting soil samples.

The stub wings not only provided the advantage of unloading the main rotor in forward flight, but they also caused the problem that they "destroyed" part of the lift during low-speed flight or in a hover. Experiments were therefore carried out with shortened stub wings, and these were used on modern versions such as the Mi-24PN and Mi-35M. The shortened stub wings had just two pylons, but the downturned wingtips were gone. All the pylons were now capable of carrying quadruple launchers for guided antitank missiles.

The stub wings were shortened again on the civil Mi-24PS for disaster relief. They had space for just one pylon per wing (two total), which as a rule were used for fuel tanks.

Beginning with the Mi-24V version, flare dispensers were mounted on both sides of the aft fuselage at the factory. Three dispensers were carried per side as a rule, and there were variants with and without aerodynamic fairings.

From the Mi-24V version, a platform was introduced above the aft fuselage that was supposed to carry an active infrared-jamming system (Lipa, Ispanka). The infrared-jamming system proved so

The shortened stub wing of modern versions of the Mi-24. *Rostvertol PLC*

effective in Afghanistan that older versions of the Mi-24 were retrofitted with the system.

Modern Mi-35Ms were equipped with sensors to detect missile launches. The sensors react to the flash when a missile is fired, and warn the crew, who can initiate countermeasures. The system could also be set so that the helicopter's computer automatically initiated countermeasures after receipt of the warning report.

Under the Mi-24's fuselage there was a mounting point on which hooks for the transport of external loads up to a maximum of 4,400 pounds (5,290 pounds for the Mi-35M) could be attached.

The fuselage ended in the removable tail boom, which had an elliptical cross section and was braced by eleven formers. It transitioned into a tail fin with a sweep angle of 42.3 degrees.

The flare dispenser mounted on this Mi-24P has an aerodynamic fairing. The Ispanka IR jammer has a protective cover. *Normann*

Flare dispenser without aerodynamic fairing on a Russian Mi-35M. *Rostvertol PLC*

ABOVE: Tail boom of a Venezuelan Mi-35M with various antennas. *Sergio J. Padrón A. via Rostvertol PLC*

LEFT: Another arrangement of the flare dispensers with no aerodynamic fairing. *Rostvertol PLC*

The aerodynamically shaped tail fin of the Mi-24D. *Normann*

Most versions of the Mi-24 used three-blade tail rotors. *Normann*

X-shaped tail rotor on the Mi-35M. *Rostvertol PLC*

The tail fin was aerodynamically shaped so that in forward flight, it compensated for a significant part of the torque produced by the main rotor, and unloaded the tail rotor. At maximum speed the tail fin produced two-thirds of the necessary torque balance, and the tail rotor one-third. The Mi-24A's tail rotor was initially mounted on the starboard side of the tail fin and functioned as a push rotor. The last production batch of Mi-24As was fitted with a revised tail fin with the rotor on the port side, with its direction of rotation reversed. The new tail rotor henceforth worked as a pull rotor directly in the rotor stream of the main rotor and was therefore more effective. The tail rotor was a three-blade design. Its structure was similar to that of the main rotor; however, each segment consisted mainly of glass fiber composite. The tail rotor could be deiced electrically, exactly like the main rotor.

The Mi-35M uses the X-shaped tail rotor of the Mi-28. The unusual shape of this tail rotor, which apart from the Mi-28 is seen only on the American AH-64 Apache, is supposed to reduce noise levels. The reduction of the helicopter's flight noise, most of which is produced by the tail rotor, reduces the distance from which the Mi-35M can be heard.

The tail skid was supposed to prevent the tail boom from striking the ground. *Normann*

Under the Mi-24's tail fin is a massive tail skid, which is supposed to prevent the tail bearer from striking the ground and fatal contact between the tail rotor and the ground during takeoff and landing.

On both sides of the tail boom are two stabilizers, whose purpose is to improve the helicopter's longitudinal stability. They are controllable and move synchronously with the collective.

Both stabilizers were movable. *Normann*

The circular objects on the underside of the tail boom are the antennas of the radio altimeter. *MLM via Mambour*

Control of the Mi-24 takes place via control rods and cables. Hydraulic amplifiers are present to reduce control loads, and both roll control and pitch control are trimmable. Yaw control has a pedal damper.

On the tail boom there are radio antennas. The antennas for the radio altimeter and the Doppler navigation system were mounted on the underside.

A block of four launchers for signal rockets was present from the beginning.

In contrast, the flare dispensers were retrofitted, being attached at the end of the tail boom by tension bands. At first there were two dispensers, one firing to port and the other to starboard. The number of dispensers was later raised to four, with two firing in each direction.

When the installation of flare dispensers became standard on the Mi-24V and later versions, the retrofitting of flare dispensers was no longer necessary.

The antenna arrangement on the Mi-24D. *Normann*

Antenna arrangement on a Czech Mi-24V. *Normann*

Flare dispensers retrofitted to an Mi-24D. *Normann Collection*

Antenna arrangement on a Venezuelan Mi-35M. *Sergio J. Padrón A. via Rostvertol PLC*

Radio Equipment

The Mi-24D's radio equipment consisted of R-863 and Karat-24 radio sets. In addition, it is equipped with an R-852 emergency receiver, and the pilot's rescue equipment includes an R-855UM emergency radio.

The R-863 was used for radio communications in the quasi-optical range. The radio operated in the 100 to 150 MHz (AM medium wave) and 220 to 400 MHz (FM ultrashort wave) frequency bands, with channel separation of 25 MHz. A total of 9,200 frequencies could be selected, of which twenty can be preset in the radio set.

Switching from one channel to another took about one and a half seconds.

The radio's range was dependent on the helicopter's altitude.

The R-863 also included an emergency receiver, which was set on the international emergency frequency of 121.5 MHz. The radio's blade antenna was located on the helicopter's tail boom.

The Karat-24 radio system was designed for communication in the medium- and long-wave bands. Karat-24 operated in a frequency band from 2 to 10.1 MHz, with channel separation of 1 MHz. In total, 8,100 channels could be selected, although just one channel could be preselected on this radio. The transmitting power of the Karat-24 was three times as great as the R-863; however, switching from channel to channel took about five seconds.

Two wire antennas leading from the fuselage to the stabilizing fins on the tail boom were used with this radio.

The R-852 emergency radio was part of the AKR-U2 VHF radio compass. It was set to the emergency radio frequency 121.5 MHz, but it could also be set to other frequencies. The R-852 radio had its own antenna (aft blade antenna) on the Mi-24's tail boom, but it also simultaneously used the R-863 radio's antenna (forward blade antenna).

The pilot's personal equipment included the R-855UM emergency radio set. It was used to establish communications between the pilot of a helicopter in distress and search-and-rescue forces and transmitted on 121.5 MHz, the international emergency frequency. For practice purposes, equipment was used whose frequency was set to 121.7 MHz.

In total, four permanently set frequencies could be used to communicate with search-and-rescue forces. The range of the R-855UM was dependent on the altitude of the search helicopter and the topographical features in the area. Under ideal conditions, voice communications could be established from 28 miles over land and 32 miles over water.

Voice communications between two R 855UM radios could as a rule bridge distances between 1.9 and 3.1 miles on the water and about 0.6 miles on land. Communications were possible at up to 6.2 miles with the use of a 25-foot-long mast antenna.

The emergency radio could transmit a continuous signal to allow the search-and-rescue forces to home in on it.

The R-855UM's packaging was watertight and shockproof. The radio functioned even when submerged in up to 3 feet of water.

Radio Compass

The ARK-15 automatic radio compass was a simple navigation system that indicated the direction to a nondirectional beacon. With the help of the ARK-15, the pilot could home in on medium-wave transmitters, whether a radio beacon, radio marker, emergency radio station, or commercial radio station. The usable frequency range was 1.5 to 180 MHz.

The radio compass indicator in an Mi-24D. *Normann*

The ARK-15 enabled the crew of the Mi-24 to set course directly to the beacon or, by homing in on several beacons, to triangulate its position.

The ARK-15 indicator was located in the pilot's cockpit of the Mi-24.

The ARK-2U radio compass was used mainly for SAR purposes, meaning searching for, locating, and rescuing crews in distress. It operated in the frequency range of 100 to 150 MHz and was interconnected with the R-852 aircraft radio.

Radio Altimeter and Doppler Navigation System

The Mi-24 was equipped with an RV-5 radio altimeter. The antennas for the device, which operated in continuous wave mode, were located on the underside of the tail boom. By measuring the elapsed time between transmission of the radio signal and receipt of its reflection from the surface of the earth, the exact height above ground could be determined and indicated. By using the Doppler effect, the DISS-15

The Doppler navigation system's indicator device in the Mi-24D.
Normann

Doppler navigation system could also determine airspeed and drift angle. It was thus possible, coming from a known point, to navigate accurately on the basis of actual movements over the ground.

Using the altitude, airspeed, and heading information received, it calculated the helicopter's actual position and displayed this with the help of an indicator system (crosshair) on an instrument in the pilot's cockpit.

Prior to takeoff, a flight map had to be entered in the indicator and the scale of the map set, with maps in scales of 1:1,000,000 and more being used for general orientation rather than a precise determination of position. Precise position determinations were possible with 1:200,000 scale maps.

TV3-117 Engine

The TV3-117 engine was developed in the Klimov design bureau in Leningrad between 1965 and 1972 under the leadership of engineers Isotov and Lyunevich. It was based on the earlier TV2-117, which proved itself exceptionally well in the Mi-8.

The abbreviation TV stood for *Turbovalniy Dvigatyel* (Турбовальный двигатель), which can be translated as turboshaft engine. The number "3" defines the engine type; the number "117," the design bureau.

The engines of the TV3-117 family weighed between 628 and 650 pounds. They were 81 inches long, 25 inches wide, and 28 inches tall and were not self-starting; an AI-9V auxiliary power unit was needed to start them.

The TV3-117's fuel consumption was between 0.47 and 0.5 pounds per horsepower-hour. Depending on version, takeoff power varied between 2,000 and 2,500 hp. Emergency power, which was available for a brief period, was significantly greater.

The TV3-117 was air cooled. As of 1975, dust covers were mounted that were supposed to prevent the ingestion of large foreign objects. The inlet guide vanes were located in the engine's air intake. Its blades were adjustable depending on revolutions.

This was followed by an axial compressor, whose purpose was to compress incoming air and thus increase pressure. The TV3-117's axial compressor had twelve stages. The guide vanes of the first four stages of the axial compressor were adjusted automatically on the basis of revolutions. The number of blades per rotor increased with each compressor

A modern engine of the TV3-117 family. *Motor Sich*

stage to deal with the constantly changing pressure and flow conditions.

The axial compressor was followed by an annular combustion chamber with twelve injection nozzles. Here, fuel and air were mixed and then burned. The first part of the combustion chamber was called the diffuser. It ensured that the speed of the incoming air remained constant. It was flowed by the flame tube; air was blown into the flame tube via twelve nozzles. The injection nozzles added fuel to the airflow, producing a flammable air-fuel mixture that was ignited and burned.

Part of the airflow was also diverted around the flame tube. In part this was used for cooling, but in the further course of the flame tube there were additional openings through which air could stream into the flame tube. This was intended to ensure a constant supply of oxygen and, associated with it, stable burning of the fuel in the entire burn zone of the flame tube.

The annular combustion chamber was followed by a two-stage axial turbine (compressor turbine), which powered the axial compressor by way of an air-cooled shaft. Since the shaft had to pass through

the annular combustion chamber to the compressor, it was exposed to high thermal loads. To counter this, cooling air was bled from several compressor stages and blown directly into the shaft.

Following the compressor turbine there was a second two-stage axial turbine, which delivered the actual power for propulsion via a shaft to the main transmission. The two turboshafts were not rigidly connected but instead were coupled together by gas dynamics. The second axial turbine is called the free turbine.

After passing through the free turbine, the stream of exhaust gases passed through the curved exhaust pipe to the outside. The exhaust tube was double walled; cooling air streamed between the two walls. The free turbine's shaft ran through the middle of the bend in the exhaust pipe. Placed between the exhaust pipe and the main reduction gearing, the drive shaft had a rated breakpoint, which in the case of mechanical problems in the transmission was supposed to interrupt the transmission of power.

Testing of the AVU system for cooling and dispersing exhaust gases began in 1982. Starting in 1984, all TV3-117s were prepared at the factory for fitting of the AVU.

Quantity production of the TV3-117 began in 1972 at the Motorstoytyel Factory in the Ukrainian city of Zaporozhye, now Motor Sich (Russian: Мотор Сич; Ukrainian: Мотор Січ).

Since then, more than 25,000 engines of the TV3-117 family have been built, accumulating a total operating time of more than sixteen million flying hours. They were and are used in the Mi-24, the Mi-14 naval helicopter, and the transport helicopters of the Mi-8 / Mi-17 family.

Representatives of the company that makes the engine are proud of the statement that the TV3-117 engines are among the most widely used and reliable helicopter engines in the world, and justifiably so.

TV3-117

The original engine was built in four series, which were continually improved. It was optimized for operation near ground level.

0 series	Introductory series of sixty engines for Mi-24 trials
1st series	Improved variant, about 200 built for the Mi-24A
2nd series	Improved variant, about 2,000 built for the Mi-24A and D
3rd series	Built in large numbers from 1977 onward

Empty weight	628 pounds
Fuel consumption	0.49 pounds per horsepower-hour
Emergency power 2.5 minutes	2,000 hp (one engine only)
Maximum power for thirty minutes	2,000 hp
Normal power	1,500 hp

A brief maximum output of 2,200 hp was possible for engines of the 3rd series.

TV3-117V

The TV3-117V was a version optimized for use at higher altitudes and in mountainous regions. It was developed at Zaporozhye in a short time under the leadership of A. S. Krasnikov. The engine entered series production at the end of 1980. The TV3-117V was initially produced primarily for all the attack helicopters deployed in Afghanistan, but later all models of the Mi-24 were equipped with this engine.

The power curve of the TV3-117V was changed so that the engine produced more power at higher altitudes. To achieve this, the performance curve was raised from sea level to 6,561 feet. Takeoff power was restricted to 2,073 hp to avoid overstraining the engines, which were governed electrically. In an extreme emergency the performance governor could be turned off, allowing the TV3-117V to reach up to 2,059 hp. This enormous increase in power when the governor was turned off led to heavy wear and a sharp reduction in operating life. There was also the danger of overstressing the helicopter's main transmission.

Empty weight	628 pounds
Fuel consumption	0.49 pounds per horsepower-hour
Emergency power 2.5 minutes	2,100 hp (one engine only)
Maximum power for thirty minutes	2,100 hp
Maximum power with governor turned off	2,800 hp

TV3-117VM

The TV3-117VM was a modernization variant equipped with an automatic emergency regime. The engine could deliver a maximum output of 2,000 hp up to an altitude of 11,800 feet. Production began in 1986.

Empty weight	648 pounds
Fuel consumption	0.48 pounds per horsepower-hour
Emergency power 2.5 minutes	2,200 hp (one engine only)
Maximum power for thirty minutes	2,100 hp
Normal power	1,500 hp
Maximum Power with governor turned off	2,800 hp

TV3-117VMA

The TV3-117VMA was a modification of the VM. The *A* stood for *Series A* of the TV3-117VM. It was capable of produced greater power in the emergency regime than its predecessor.

Empty weight	648 pounds
Fuel consumption	0.47 pounds per horsepower-hour
Emergency power 2.5 minutes	2,400 hp (one engine only)
Maximum power for thirty minutes	2,200 hp
Normal power	1,500 hp

TV3-117VMA-SBM1

The SBM1 was an improved variant of the VMA developed in the Ukraine. It entered production in 2010. Exports to Russia, the former principal customer, were halted for political reasons. Today the TV3-117VMA-SBM1 is the standard engine in Ukrainian helicopters and is offered worldwide as part of an Mi-17 and Mi-24 modernization program.

Empty weight	650 pounds
Fuel consumption	0.49 pounds per horsepower-hour
Emergency power 2.5 minutes	2,800 hp (one engine only)
Maximum power for thirty minutes	2,500 hp
Normal power	1,750 hp

VK-2500

As part of the effort to make itself independent of the potentially unreliable Ukraine as its supplier of helicopter engines, in the first decade of the twenty-first century, Russia began building up its own engine production. First they assembled engines from Ukrainian components. At the same time, OAO Klimov began developing its own improved versions of the TV3-117VMA. These variants were designated VK-2500. VK stands for Vassily Klimov, the founding father of the design bureau, while "2500" symbolizes the projected horsepower.

Development of the engine was initially kept on the back burner, but when political relations with the Ukraine deteriorated after the election of a pro-Western government in Kiev, the pace of development rose and the engine was approved in 2012. Series production of a VK-2500 engine made exclusively of Russian parts began in 2014. Annual production is forecast to rise to 350 engines by 2017. New-build Russian helicopters use this engine, and it is also exported.

The VK-2500-2 and VK-2500M are more-powerful variants.

Empty weight	650 pounds
Fuel consumption	0.49 pounds per horsepower-hour
Emergency power 2.5 minutes	2,700 hp (one engine only)
Maximum power for thirty minutes	2,400 hp
Normal power	1,750 hp

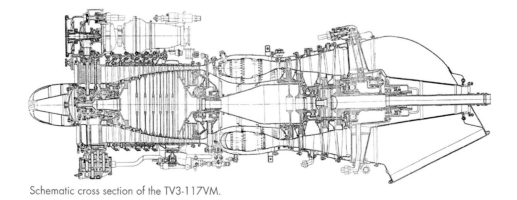

Schematic cross section of the TV3-117VM.

This TV3-117 is on display at Hermeskeil. *Alf van Beem*

TV3-117 seen from behind. *Alf van Beem*

The Armament of the Mi-24

Cannon / Machine Guns

Afanasyev A-12.7 (9A016P)

The A-12.7 heavy machine gun was developed by chief designer Nikolai Mikhailovich Afanasyev in Central Design Bureau No. 14 (ZKB-14) between 1949 and 1953 under the project designation TBK-481 (ТКБ-481). The weapon was produced from 1953 until 1983.

The A-12.7 was originally envisaged as armament for the Tu-4 bomber but was later used on helicopters as well. It was first used as standard equipment on the Mi-4. It also saw use on the attack helicopter variant of the Mi-8 (Mi-8TB).

The single-barrel A-12.7 heavy machine gun was a gas-operated self-loader weighing 56 pounds, which was designed for the 12.7 × 108 mm cartridge. The prototype of the weapon had a theoretical rate of fire of about 1,400 rounds per minute, but to extend the life of the weapon the rate of fire was lowered to 800 to 1,100 rounds per minute. The A-12.7 was capable of engaging targets up to a distance of 3,937 feet.

Since the intended main armament of the Mi-24, the Yak-B machine gun, was not ready for service in time, OKB Mil decided to use the A-12.7 as an interim solution. The weapon was used on the Mi-24A, the first production variant.

Yakushev-Borzov Yak-B-12.7 (9A624)

In 1968, the Central Design Bureau for Hunting and Sporting Weapons, situated in the old armory town of Tula, was given the task of developing a rapid-firing machine gun by the leadership of the Soviet tactical air forces. This weapon would find use as part of the armament of attack helicopters.

In its tactical-technical requirements, the military demanded a weapon in the common caliber of 12.7 mm, designed to use the powerful and widespread M30/38 12.7 × 108 mm cartridge. Rate of fire was to be in the area of 4,000 to 5,000 rounds per minute,

Yak-B-12.7 and Yak-BJu-12.7 machine guns in the weapons museum in Tula. *Scheffler Collection*

The Yak-B-12.7 rotary machine gun was mounted in the Mi-24's USPU-24 revolving turret. *Mambour*

with a barrel life of 8,000 to 10,000 rounds. The prescribed weight of the weapon was 66 pounds.

A corresponding technical project was developed under the leadership of Pyotr Gerasimovich Yakushev, and in December 1968 it was approved by the military. The subsequently developed prototype of the weapon was given the designation TKB-063 (ТКБ-063).

The TKB-063 was a machine gun that operated on the Gatling principle, having four barrels that rotated about its longitudinal axis. It was a gas-operated self-loader, so that in contrast to Western rotary weapons, no external drive was necessary. This design had the advantage that the maximum firing rate was achieved very quickly. A disadvantage of self-powered

rotary weapons is that failure of the ammunition to ignite results in the immediate cessation of fire. To overcome jams, there were two pyro cartridges with which the mechanism could be restarted.

Ammunition was delivered by an ammunition belt consisting of disintegrating links.

Initial firing trials with the weapon took place in March 1970, which showed that barrel life was far below the requested norm. To solve this problem, the barrel liners were coated with a cobalt alloy and used cartridges with a weaker powder load.

During subsequent testing of the TKB-063, which extended through 1971, there were repeated problems related to the weapon's reliability. Overcoming this problem proved difficult and time consuming, and testing went on into 1972. In September 1962, modified

The servicing hatches are closed after the ammunition has been loaded. *US Army, Angelita Lawrence*

TKB-063 guns successfully completed factory trials. Three sample copies of the weapon were subsequently released for state trials. Testing lasted from September 1972 until August 1973. After these successful ground tests the weapon was approved for installation in an airborne weapons system, and flight testing began.

Despite these positive results, designers Yakushev and Borzov were not really satisfied with the TKB-063. The design of the TKB-063 was still quite far from being a robust and reliable weapon of war, in part because the weapon's design was very complicated. For example, for each barrel there was an independent

gas piston system for the purpose of power transmission. Although the individual components worked reliably by themselves, because of the complex structure the overall reliability of the weapons system was clearly limited. To reduce the complexity the weapon had to be greatly simplified.

In December 1972, two prototypes with simplified design were built in Tula. The power system now consisted of just twelve instead of eighty-eight individual parts. Instead of four gas pistons, now there was just one, which during firing moved back and forth between two gas chambers and thus produced the necessary energy to power the rotation mechanism. The new system functioned satisfactorily.

In May 1973, the weapon was tested under different temperature conditions.

That same year, Pyotr Yakushev died and his deputy Boris Afanasyevich Borzov took over the task of completing testing of the new weapon and putting it into production. And that was no simple task.

Fine-tuning the gas piston mechanism and the associated continuous rate of fire went on into 1974. Even before this task was completed, in June 1973 the manufacturing factory was ordered to prepare for production of the TKB-063. Production was expected to begin in July 1974.

Flight testing of the TKB-063 took place between 1975 and 1977 onboard Mi-24B and Mi-24D helicopters. The weapon was installed both in a chin turret and in a cannon pod on one of the stub wings. The chin turret was the USPU-24, which was controlled from the cockpit. The USPU-24 enabled the weapon to be traversed ± 60 degrees. It could also be moved in elevation 20 degrees up and 40 degrees down.

The gunner, the second member of the helicopter crew, was primarily responsible for operating the machine gun. He aimed by using a KPS-53AV targeting device in the cockpit. The resulting values were fed to the VSB-24 weapons computer by an encoder, It calculated the weapon's directional angle and positioned the USPU-24 chin turret. The gunner had to press both firing buttons on the targeting device to fire the cannon.

In an emergency the pilot could use the machine gun, but it first had to be locked in the neutral position.

The cannon used B-32 and BST-44 ammunition.

The TKB-063 was accepted for service in the Soviet armed services by the Council of Ministers of the USSR in March 1976. The official type designation was changed to Yakushev-Borzov YaK-B 12.7 (9A624) (ЯкБ-12,7 (9А624) конструкции Якушева-Борзова).

In peacetime and under shooting-range conditions, the Yak-B proved to be a reliable weapon. Its first hard test, however, was the Soviet war in Afghanistan, during which the machine gun revealed several weaknesses that had not come to light during testing. Not until under the extreme conditions in Afghanistan was it revealed that some parts of the weapon worked near their sustainable thermal and physical limits. Overheating, which could lead to shooting hot and resulting jams, was the order of the day. Occasionally there even were cases of ammunition in the chamber self-igniting, leading to uncontrolled firing of the weapon.

To prevent these problems, many units reduced the amount of ammunition carried by the Mi-24 from 1,470 rounds to just 400–500. The pilots saw this as suboptimal because the Yak-B's high rate of fire (4,000 rounds per minute) meant that this amount was used up within six to seven and a half seconds. The gunners were therefore directed to limit themselves to short bursts of a maximum of half a second in duration. It was also problematic that the weapon proved less robust when dirty than other Soviet firearms. For this reason, too, the weapon jammed frequently.

Although the Yak-B was capable of engaging targets up to a distance of about 3,937 feet, in the Hindu Kush the weapon was used mainly at shorter distances. Up to a range of 2,625 to 3,280 feet, the weapon was very accurate and was devastatingly effective. Veterans of the Afghanistan war report that soft vehicles were literally cut in half by fire from the Yak-B.

Despite all the problems that arose, mounted in the Mi-24 the Yak-B was an efficient weapon, valued by friends and feared by the foe.

In 1977, the engineers in Tula began working on a developed version of the machine gun. The goal of their efforts was to improve the weapon's reliability and increase its life. The armed forces, however, initially saw no reason to act.

This changed in 1980, after the first combat experience in Afghanistan. The leadership of the Soviet armed services now demanded that the Yak-B be changed so as to be able to fire at least half the ammunition load of an Mi-24 (750 rounds) in sustained fire without pauses to cool the weapon. The dependability and operational safety of the Yak-B were also supposed to be improved. A corresponding tactical-technical order was issued.

The machine gun's problems were subsequently put through an in-depth theoretical and practical analysis. The weapon was redesigned, which was followed by intensive testing under realistic conditions, both by the manufacturer and the state. The work was time consuming and was hindered by the burgeoning chaos of perestroika. It was not completed until late 1987. In January 1988, the modernized version, designated Yakushev Borzov Yurichev YakBYu-12.7 (ЯкБЮ-12,7 конструкции Якушева, Борзова Юрищева) was accepted into service of the Soviet armed forces by decree of the defense minister. Quantity production began.

The YakBYu-12.7 was so designed that it could replace the former Yak-B in the Mi-24's USPU-24 chin turret with only minor conversion work, even though the weapon, which now weighed 132 pounds, was 13 pounds heavier than the earlier version. The increase in weight was the result of more-massive barrels, which alone were responsible for 28 pounds of the additional weight, and the technical measures taken to divert the thermal energy created when the gun was fired.

As of 1988, the YakBYu became the standard weapon in new-built Mi-24V helicopters. Older machines were gradually retrofitted with the new weapon.

Gryazev-Shipunov GSh-23 (9A472)

The Gryazev-Shipunov GSh-23 (ГШ-23) was a twin-barreled 23 mm aircraft cannon that operated on the twin-barrel principle developed by Karl Gast in 1916. When fired, the weapon shot from one barrel while the second barrel was loaded simultaneously. This process repeated itself alternately and continuously. It thus combined a comparatively high rate of fire with a relatively simple design.

The GSh-23 was developed on the basis of lessons learned in the Korean War. There, with their low rate of fire, the automatic cannon installed in the MiG-15 had proved less than ideal for engaging highly maneuverable targets. Pilots returning from the war demanded a cannon with a higher rate of fire. The armed services then issued a technical requirement for a future aircraft cannon with a rate of fire of at least 2,000 rounds per minute.

The TKB-613 project was created in the arsenal in Tula. The first test examples of the new weapon were produced in 1954 and underwent extensive factory trials. Several weaknesses were found and corrected. The firing mechanism alone had to be redesigned five times, until it finally achieved the required level of reliability. Work on the weapon went on for five years. In 1959, it was decided to place the TKB-613 into production under the designation Gryazev-Shipunov GSh-23 (9A472).

Under operational conditions, the first production cannon revealed an unsatisfactorily short operating life, and several changes to the design were necessary. Work on these improvements went on for half a decade, and the GSh-23 did not officially enter service until 1965.

Afterward the GSh-23 became the standard Soviet aircraft cannon and was installed in many aircraft types. In combat it proved to be a reliable and potent weapon.

In principle the double-barreled GSh-23's general structure consisted of two individual automatic cannon that shared a common housing, a common gas pressure system for reloading the weapon, and a common ammunition feed and firing mechanism. The automatic-reloading systems of both weapons were so connected that the gas pressure produced when one cannon was fired powered the automatic reload of the other cannon. This ensured that only one barrel fired while the other had time to reload. In this way a denser curtain of fire was created, as if both barrels were firing simultaneously.

Since all the movements by the individual weapons parts took place along the weapon's longitudinal axis, there was less vibration than in other weapons with rotating components (Gatling or revolver cannon), which enabled more-accurate firing. The maximum operational firing range of the GSh-23 was about 6,560 feet.

The weapons ammunition was fed by a disintegrating belt. A star-shaped mechanism pulled the individual cartridges from the belt and fed them into the chambers of the automatic cannon. The ammunition that was used had a caliber of 23 × 115 mm. There were armor-piercing napalm canister rounds, armor-piercing napalm canister rounds with tracer, high-explosive fragmentation rounds, high-explosive fragmentation rounds with tracer, and radar-jamming rounds with chaff. East German pilots reported that shells without tracer were used as combat ammunition as a rule.

Gryazev-Shipunov GSh-30-2K (9A623K)

The GSh-30-2 (ГШ-30-2) was also designated GSh-2-30 or GSh-302. It was a twin-barreled aircraft cannon that was closely related to the GSh-23. Like the earlier weapon, the GDh-30-2 operated on the principle of alternating fire by two barrels developed by Karl Gast.

The GSh-30-2 (9A623) was created during development of the MiG-29. The military demanded a fast-firing cannon with greater penetrative ability and more destructive power for the next generation

The GSh-23L of a Brazilian Mi-35M. *Clausio Lucchesi via Rostvertol PLC*

Clausio Lucchesi via Rostvertol PLC

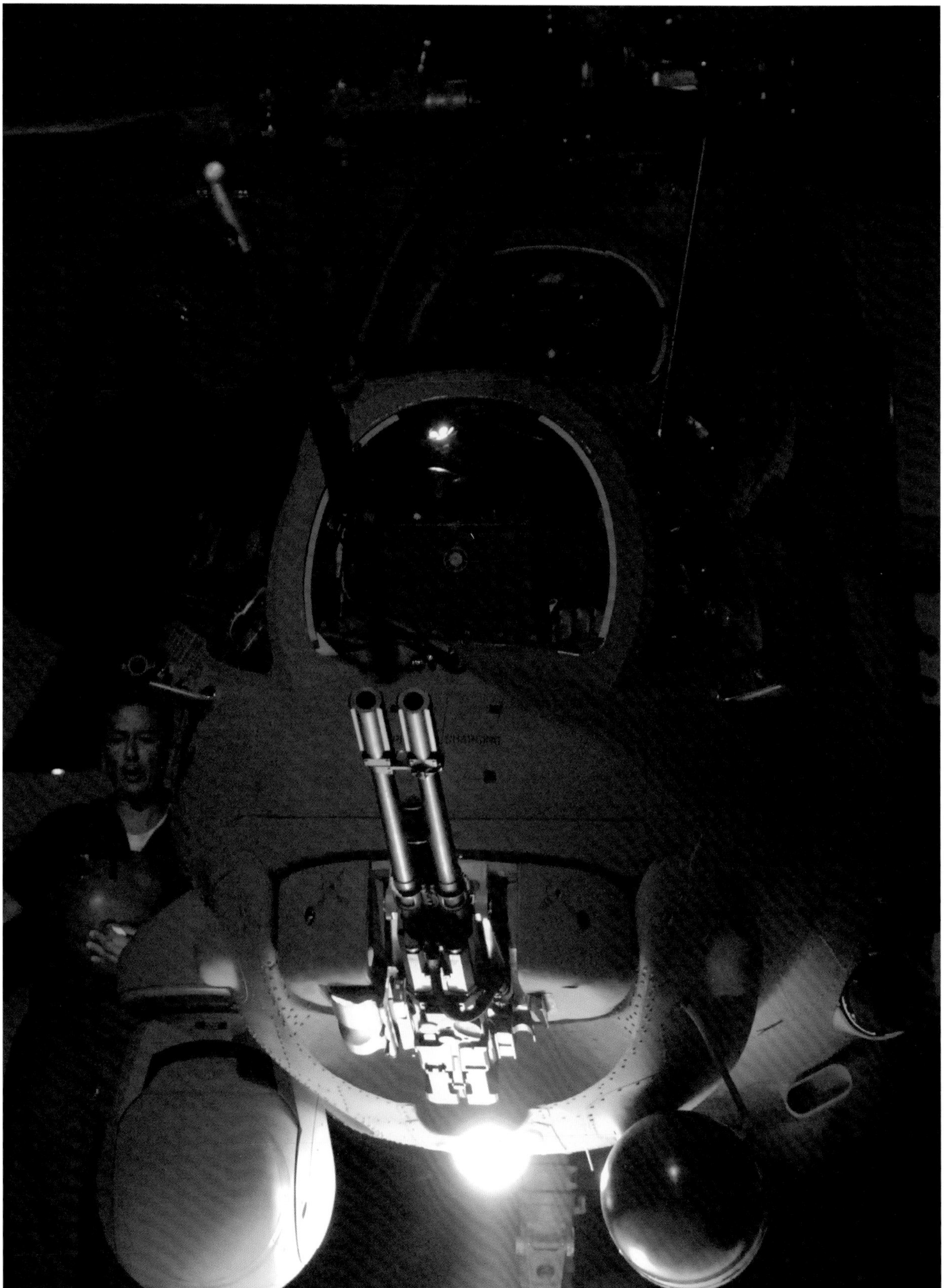

of fighter aircraft. Since the GSh-23's design had proved itself in combat, the answer to the problem was seen to be to redesign the weapon in a larger-caliber: 30 mm was selected as the caliber, and the newly developed 30 × 165 mm cartridge was suggested as its ammunition. The military command hoped to create a standard cartridge for all future 30 mm automatic cannon and to simplify logistics. Today this cartridge is used by all branches of service. It is used by 30 mm cannon mounted on armored personnel carriers and antiaircraft tanks, the 30 mm rotary cannon of the naval artillery, and the cannon in all modern Soviet/Russian combat aircraft.

During development of the MiG-29, the designers decided to abandon the GSh-30-2 for weight reasons and replace it with the lighter, single-barrel GSh-301. However, the GSh-30-2 proved to be the ideal weapon for the T-8 close-support aircraft project, which Sukhoi was developing on the back burner. Initially rejected by the military, the T-8 would undergo intensive operational trials in Afghanistan. It was found to be an effective close-support aircraft and was immediately put into production as the Su-25.

Since there were problems with the machine gun armament of the Mi-24, the Mil OKB looked into the possibility of integrating the GSh-30-2 into the Mi-24's weapons system. In principle a fixed installation parallel to the aircraft's longitudinal axis was considered possible; however, the penetrative power of the GSh-30-2 left something to be desired. No problems had arisen with the penetrative power of the shells when used by the fast-flying Su-25, since the speed of the aircraft added to the weapon's muzzle velocity, giving the shells additional kinetic energy. The Mi-24 flew much slower, however. It was therefore decided to modify the GSh-30-2 and equip it with longer barrels. Believe it or not, the weapon's length grew by 35 inches, and its weight rose from 231 to 278 pounds. Muzzle velocity rose from 2,854 to 3,084 feet per second, with a corresponding improvement in penetrative ability. The new variant was given the designation GSh-30-2K.

To make the cannon better suited for use in an attack helicopter, the Tula weapons developers equipped the GSh-30-2 with a rate-of-fire regulator. For the precise shelling of targets it could be lowered to a rate of fire of 300 to 400 rounds per minute. Normally, however, the weapon was fired in rapid-fire mode of 2,000 to 2,600 rounds per minute.

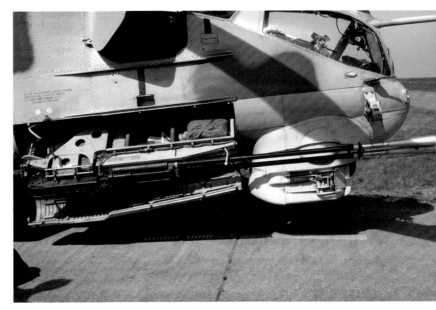

The GSh-30-2K can be lowered for servicing of the weapon and reloading. During transfer flights, pilots like to use the space for the ammunition to transport personal effects. *Mambour*

The filled magazine space of the Mi-24P. *Feller via Mambour*

To prevent the gun from overheating when fired and to lengthen the weapon's life, the designers fitted the GSh-30-2 with a liquid cooling system. This system cools the body of the weapon, not the barrels. In warm weather it is filled with water, while in cold conditions the addition of 40 percent alcohol is prescribed.

To protect the attack helicopter's nose from muzzle blast, the weapon's muzzles are fitted with funnel-shaped muzzle flash compensators. They also prevent the crew from being blinded by the muzzle flash.

The GSh-30-2K's rate of fire is much lower than that of the Yak-B or GSh-23. It makes up for this disadvantage through its clearly greater weight of fire. The effect on the target is correspondingly greater.

Unguided Rockets

S-5

The S-5 rocket was created as the Soviet response to the German R4M unguided air-to-air rocket, which was used against American heavy bombers. The 57 mm (2.2 inch) S-5 rocket was intended to counter the threat posed by the nuclear bombers of a potential enemy. It was envisaged that fighter aircraft would be vectored onto the incoming enemy aircraft so that they could shower the bombers with a hail of rockets and destroy them.

Development of the rocket and its launch pod began in the early 1950s. Rockets and pod were envisaged as armament for the OKB MiG's first supersonic fighter, which carried the interim designation SM, which entered service as the MiG-19. The S-5 rocket was carried in a PRO-57K pod.

Although unguided rockets lacked accuracy, in many cases they did in fact bring down enemy aircraft. The most spectacular case was the shooting down of an American RB-66 reconnaissance aircraft over a major Soviet maneuver near the city of Gardelegen in 1964.

With the advent of guided air-to-air missiles, the S-5 was forced into the role of an air-to-surface rocket. For the most efficient possible use of the rockets, larger pods holding more rockets were developed. These included the standard UB-16 and UB-32 pods, and the Mars-2 pod (developed in Poland).

The S-5R design consisted of a steel tube with a solid-fuel engine and nozzle in one end. The rocket engine had a burn duration of about 1.1 seconds, which

UB-32 rocket pod. *Normann*

was sufficient to carry the rocket over a maximum combat range of about 1.9 miles. At the end of the rocket engine, just in front of the nozzle, were eight folding fins that extended rearward. They deployed after the rocket was fired, and gave the projectile a stable rotation movement around its longitudinal axis.

The forward part of the rocket was filled with the warhead, including the fuse.

There were many different warheads for the S-5. They ranged from pure fragmentation warheads with impact fuses, to hollow-charge heads with additional fragmentation casings and piezoelectric fuses, to radar decoys and battlefield illumination warheads.

The S-5, together with its UB-16 and UB-32 pods, has been used in a multitude of military conflicts. Thanks to the rocket pods' high rate of fire, they are quite suitable for engaged soft-area targets. Their penetrative capability against armored targets leaves something to be desired, however. For this reason the S-5 was gradually replaced by the more powerful S-8 rocket.

Launching rockets. *US Army, Shank*

Air-Ground Variants			
Type	**Warhead**	**Notes**	**Number of Fragments**
S-5K (S-5K1)	hollow charge	150 mm steel	—
S-5KO	hollow charge / fragmentation	170 mm steel	220
S-5KPB	hollow charge / fragmentation	250 mm steel	?
S-5M (S-5M1)	fragmentation	—	75
S-5MO	fragmentation	—	360
S-5S	fléchette	—	1,000
S-5P1	chaff	radar decoy	
S-5O1	magnesium	illuminant for 15–25 sec. battlefield illumination	

Development of the S-8 rocket began in the late 1960s, with the objective of creating a more powerful alternative to the widely used S-5. Desired was an increase in the number of fragments, improved penetrative ability of the hollow-charge warheads, longer range, and better thermal stability to allow higher speeds by the carrying aircraft. Since the danger always existed that exhaust gases from the rocket might enter the air intake of the aircraft and cause engine failure, measures were also demanded to prevent such an occurrence from happening.

This was achieved by development of the new B-8M, B-8M1, and B-8V7 rocket pods. The first pod held twenty 80 mm (3.15 inch) S-8 rockets, while the B-8V7 carried just seven rockets. The B-8W20A and B-8-10 pods were developed for use by attack helicopters.

The S-8 rocket was similar in design to the S-5. It also consisted of a steel tube, this time of 80 mm caliber, with the rocket engine housed in the rear. Modernized rockets (M) were fitted with more-powerful rocket engines to increase range.

Afghan technicians loading a rocket pod. *US Army, Lawrence*

The number of stabilizing fins was reduced to six. On the S-8, spring pressure deployed them forward. In deployed condition they spanned 15 inches.

The warhead was in the forward part of the rocket. Like the S-5, the S-8 also had many different warheads. In addition to the types known from the S-5, there were antibunker, fuel-air warheads, and target markers. In total there are twenty-five different production versions of the S-8 rocket plus other experimental types.

The S-8 was integrated into the Mi-24's armaments from the Mi-24V and Mi-24P versions.

An Mi-24V firing a salvo of S-8 unguided rockets. *Rostvertol PLC*

Several Variants			
Type	Warhead	Notes	Range
S-8B / BM	concrete piercing	800 mm concrete	to 7,200 ft.
S-8D / DM	fuel-air	—	to 9,840 ft.
S-8DF	fuel-air	—	to 13,120 ft.
S-8M / KOM	hollow charge / fragmentation	400 mm steel	to 13,120 ft
S-8O	magnesium	illuminant for 30 sec. battlefield illumination	—
S-8P	chaff	radar decoy	to 9,840 ft.
S-8T	tandem hollow charge	400 mm steel behind reactive armor	to 13,120 ft.
S-8S	fléchette	2,000 arrow-shaped fragments	to 11,480 ft.
S-8ZM	smoke	target marker	to 9,840 ft.

S-13

The unguided S-13 122 mm (4.8 inch) rocket was created in the 1970s to close the gap between the relatively small-caliber S-5 and S-8 rockets and the large-caliber S-24 with a more modern rocket. This was necessary because after the lessons of the Israeli-Arab Six Day War in 1967, all military powers in Europe began housing their aircraft in hardened aircraft shelters. A sufficiently powerful unguided rocket was needed to engage enemy aircraft in their shelters. The S-24 was already available, but because of its size, Soviet fighter-bombers could carry only a few of them. This meant that it might not be possible to engage all targets on enemy airfields. A smaller-caliber rocket was therefore needed that could be carried in sufficient numbers.

Work on the S-13 (C-13) began in 1973, at the Institute for Applied Physics in Novosibirsk. Devel-

opment work went on until 1979, when the rocket and its UB-13 pod became available for testing.

Arched NATO aircraft shelters made of steel-reinforced concrete were re-created and covered with a 6-foot layer of earth, and S-13 rockets were fired at them. The results were so satisfactory that the rocket was placed into production and, in 1983, was officially added to the armament of the Soviet air forces.

Work on more-advanced warheads began in 1982 because several test shots had revealed the phenomenon of the S-13 rockets not only piercing the thin-walled aircraft bunkers but also the concrete floor within. The warhead exploded under the concrete pad but inflicted little or no damage on the actual target, the aircraft. Tandem warheads were therefore developed. The first part of the charge was supposed to pierce the outer skin of the aircraft shelter, and the second part of the charge was to explode inside the structure. In 1984, the rocket, dubbed the S-13T, was tested on Su-17M4 fighter-bombers. Ninety-nine rockets were fired in thirty-one flights. The rockets pierced 3-foot-thick concrete walls under an 18-foot layer of earth. With this performance the rockets were also capable of successfully destroying runways. During testing, 9.8-inch-thick concrete surfaces were penetrated and an area of about 172 square feet was destroyed. Maximum target deviation was 33 feet.

An armor-piercing version for engaging armored vehicles and weakly protected shelters was developed on the basis of the concrete-penetrating S-13T and was designated the S-13OF (С-13ОФ). It was also tested using Su-17M4 fighter-bombers, with retired BMP-1 armored personnel carriers serving as targets. Direct hits were not necessary to pierce the vehicles' armor. It was sufficient if an S-13OF struck within

Gravity Weapons

Bombs

The Mi-24 could carry free-fall bombs up to a weight of 1,100 pounds. The total weight of the bombload could not exceed 2,200 pounds, however.

The free-fall bombs included the FAB high-explosive bombs, which in Russian were designated *fugasnaya aviatsionnaya bomba* (Фугасные авиабомбы [ФАБ]). Explosives made up about half the bomb's weight. The remaining weight was divided among the tail fins, the fuse, and the massive bomb casing.

OFAB high-explosive fragmentation bombs (Осколочно-фугасные, ОФАБ) were also used. Soviet high-explosive fragmentation bombs differed from pure high-explosive bombs in that they had a smaller amount of explosives, in this case only about a third

Several Variants			
Type	Warhead	Notes	Range
S-13	concrete piercing	3 ft. steel concrete under 10 ft. layer of earth	to 9,840 ft.
S-13T	tandem	3 ft. steel concrete under 20 ft. layer of earth	to 13,120 ft.
S-13OF	fragmentation HE	450 large-caliber fragments	to 9,840 ft.
S-13D	fuel-air	—	to 9,840 ft.
S-13DF	fuel-air	—	to 19,685 ft.

15 feet of the armored personnel carrier. The force of the large-caliber fragments (0.9 to 1.2 ounces) pierced the armor. Not until a distance of 33 feet or more did the BMP's armor protect it in some cases. From 82 to 164 feet the BMP-1's armor protection was acceptable, and it was not until a distance of 164 feet from the point of impact by an S-13 that the vehicle was completely safe. In 1986, the S-13OF was added to the armory.

The S-13D (С-13Д) with a fuel-air (thermobaric) warhead was developed specially for the war in Afghanistan beginning in 1987. Development was not completed until 1993. The rocket entered service with the Russian military in 1995.

S-13 rockets were fired from B-13L pods housing five rockets. The B-13L1 pod was used for use from helicopters.

of the bomb's weight. It its place the designers had a prefabricated fragmentation casing. In principle this was a steel ring into which predetermined breaking points were worked. The weight of a fragment was as a rule between 0.17 and 0.35 ounces in order produce the largest possible number of fragments and to give the fragments sufficient kinetic energy to be effective even at longer ranges. Externally, Soviet high-explosive fragmentation bombs differed from high-explosive bombs in having blunt noses. This produced high drag, which quickly slowed the bomb after release. The bomb thus struck the ground almost vertically, which optimized the dispersement of fragments.

Napalm canister bombs (Зажигательная авиационная бомба, ЗАБ) contained a fire accelerant. This could be metallic thermite, crude-oil-based napalm, or white phosphorus in powder form.

High-explosive napalm canisters (фугасно-зажигательная авиационная бомба, ФЗАБ) were a combination of high-explosive and napalm canisters.

Fuel-air bombs (объёмно-детонирующая авиационная бомба, ОДАБ) are also called thermobaric or fuel-aerosol bombs. They are filled with an easily ignited fuel (gasoline or propane). On impact, a small explosive charge detonates, creating a fine, easily ignitable fuel-air mixture. A secondary delayed-action charge then ignites in order to cause the mixture to explode. The resulting shock wave has a devastating effect on simple structures and humans.

To enable the carrying aircraft or helicopter to get out of the blast effect area, the fuel-air bomb is usually equipped with a parachute.

Fuel-air bombs were used during the war in Afghanistan. They did not always function reliably, but when they did the effect was devastating. This resulted in them being referred to in soldier's jargon as "the little man's atom bomb."

KGMU Cluster Bomb

The KGMU (КМГУ, Контейнер малогабаритных грузов унифицированный) was a cluster bomb system envisaged for use by aircraft and helicopters against area targets. The KGMU was used by the Mi-24 attack helicopter beginning with the Mi-24V and Mi-24P versions.

It consisted of an aerodynamically shaped container that could be loaded with a large number of various small bombs (bomblets) and mines. These were released through four pneumatically operated doors on the underside of the container. The submunitions were ejected by spring pressure. They could be released at selected intervals, allowing different areas of ground to be engaged and adapted to different airspeeds.

Altitudes up to 3,300 feet were viewed as ideal for dropping submunitions from the KGMU. The minimum operational height was not supposed to go below 100 to 165 feet, since otherwise the area engaged would be too small.

Like all area weapons systems, the KGMU is regarded by the United Nations as a prohibited weapon; however, this has not prevented its use in a variety of conflicts.

KMGU cluster bomb container mounted on an Su-22M4. *Normann*

Weapons Pods

The Mi-24 is capable of carrying cannon and weapons pods.

The first was the UPK-23-250; this pod housed a twin-barreled GSh-23 cannon, the power supply required by this weapon, and 250 rounds of ammunition.

The second weapons pod was the GUV-8700 (9A669). This abbreviation translates as universal container for helicopters (Универсальная вертолётная гондола). The GUV can carry a variety of weapons.

The first variant of the GUV was configured as a machine gun pod. It carried a 12.7 mm Yak-B rotary

This Mi-24V is armed with UPK-23-250 cannon pods, UB-32 rocket pods, and Shturm-V guided antitank missiles. *Radomil Talk*

machine gun aligned on the longitudinal axis, with 750 rounds of ammunition. This was the same weapon used as a nose machine gun by the Mi-24D and V. Installed to the left and right of the Yak-B were two GShG-7.62 rotary machine guns with 1,800 rounds of ammunition.

The GShG-7.62 (alias TBK-621, alias 9A622) was a four-barreled, rotary, gas-operated, self-powered machine gun that was developed as a weapon for helicopters by designers Gryasev, Shipunov, and Glagolev. It entered service in 1979.

The GShG was configured for the 7.62-54R rifle cartridge. The bullets achieved a muzzle velocity of about 2,788 feet per second, and maximum firing range was 3,230 feet. It had two firing speeds: in slow operation it fired 3,500 rounds per minute, and in fast fire mode 6,000 rounds per minute.

The second variant of the GUV weapons container (some sources refer to it as GUV-1) was equipped with a 30 mm automatic AG-17A Plamya-A (9A800) grenade launcher. It carried 300 30 × 29-caliber rounds of ammunition.

GShG-7.62. *Normann Collection*

Weapon container GUW with removed machine guns
GSchaG-7.62 and JakB-12.7. *Feller via Mambour*

GUV weapons container with Plamya (flame) grenade launcher removed. *Karl-Heinz Feller via Mambour*

The Plamya automatic grenade launcher was designed as a recoil-operated weapon and could fire in single- or continuous-fire modes. Rate of fire was between fifty and five hundred shots per minute. The shells had a relatively low muzzle velocity of 606 feet per minute.

Comparison of an M43 7.62 × 39 mm cartridge used by the Kalashnikov and a grenade fired by the Plamya. *Normann Collection*

Guided Antitank Missiles

Guided antitank missiles were the main weapons system used for combating enemy tanks by almost all versions of the Mi-24.

The manually controlled Falanga-M guided antitank missile was introduced as an interim solution. It was later replaced by the semiautomatically guided Falanga-P. With the introduction of the Mi-24V the Falanga could no longer be used, and its place was taken by the newly developed Shturm-V guided antitank missile. Work on the Ataka-V guided antitank missile, which is now the standard armament of the Mi-24, began in the early 1980s.

Falanga (Phalanx)

The Falanga (Фаланга 9M11) was a first-generation guided antitank missile. It was created in the 1950s by OKB-16 under the leadership of the famous weapons designer A. Nudelman and entered production in 1960. NATO gave it the code name AT-2 Swatter.

The later Falanga-M (9M17M) was accepted by the military in 1967 and entered production in 1968. The Mi-24A was equipped with this weapon. It could also be fired from the Mi-24B and Mi-24D.

The Falanga-M was a guided missile that had to be steered to the target manually by the missile operator. This method, also called the three-point guidance method (NATO designation MCLOS, for

Manual Control to Line of Sight), requires the operator to take into account his own position, the position of the target, and the rapidly changing position of the missile. It was a very complicated procedure that demanded great finesse on the part of the operator and even more experience. Accuracy was very dependent on the ability of the operator. On average, barely a third of all missiles fired found their targets.

The next version was the Falanga-P (9M19P). This missile bridged the gap to the second generation of guided antitank missiles, since it was equipped with a semiautomatic flight control system (NATO designation SACLOS, for Semi-Automatic Command to Line of Sight).

With semiautomatic guidance the operator aimed at the target with the help of a sight and kept it covered with a reticle. At the same time, an automatic infrared direction finder tracked the missile's flight, and a goniometer measured the deviation of the missile's actual position from the sight line. A computer (in the case of the Mi-24B and D, an analog computer) calculated the control movements necessary to steer the missile to the sight line. The necessary commands were transmitted to the guided antitank missile by a radio command transmitter and executed by the missile's control surfaces. Accuracy rose to 80 percent under optimal conditions.

The Falanga-P was a 69-pound, 46-inch-long missile with a blunt, rounded nose section. Missile caliber was 5.6 inches; the span of the four control surfaces, which were in a cruciform arrangement, was 26.6 inches. The missile essentially consisted of three parts—the warhead, the equipment section, and the propulsion section.

In the propulsion section there was a single-chamber solid-fuel rocket engine that contained two half charges as propellants. The launch charge quickly accelerated the missile from 0 to 721 feet per second, while the cruise charge had the task of maintaining the missile's velocity until burnout. Also in the propulsion section were the control surface actuator group, the radio receiver system, and the flare, which made it easier for the infrared direction finder to recognize the missile.

The equipment section included the power supply, a compressed air tank, the fuse, and an electronics block. In the electronics block was a stabilization system that contained an integrated gyroscope.

Falanga guided antitank missiles. *Firkse*

The warhead was designed as a hollow charge and could penetrate a monolithic armor plate 19 to 22 inches thick at an impact angle of 90 degrees. With an impact angle of 30 degrees, the missile was still capable of penetrating an 11-inch-thick monolithic armor plate. The Falanga-P was thus capable of destroying all Western tank types in use in the 1960s and 1970s. Not until the advent of the next generation of tanks (M1 Abrams, Leopard 2) did its penetrative ability become obsolete.

The Falanga-P guided antitank missile was guided to the target by the Mi-24's gunner with the help of the Raduga-F guidance system. With the Raduga-F guidance system, the Mi-24 could use the guided antitank missile in forward flight or in a hover. During the targeting and launch phase, the two helicopter crewmen had to work together. Using his PKV sight, the pilot aimed roughly at the target and kept the helicopter in a steady flight position. The gunner aimed at the target with the guidance system's gyrostabilized sight and launched the weapon. Then, 3.5 seconds after the firing button was pressed, the missile launched and after one or two more seconds flew into the control area of the Raduga-F guidance system. Only then could the helicopter turn away from the target, with a maximum 20-degree bank and a deviation of 60 degrees from the target angle being possible. Greater course changes resulted in the loss of the missile.

The Raduga-F made it possible to observe the battlefield and identify targets at up to 16,400 feet. In scanning mode the sight magnified 3.3 times, and in targeting mode 10.0 times.

The weapon's fuse was armed about 600 feet from the helicopter. The dead zone (the area in which the missile could not yet be controlled) was 2,624 feet when fired from a hover, and 3,280 feet when fired during forward flight.

The most-favorable operational conditions for the Falanga-P were in forward flight at a height of 131 to 262 feet, at speeds between 80 and 123 mph and a combat range of 6,560 to 9,842 feet. Below 50 and above 161 mph, the helicopter vibrated significantly, which notably hampered guidance of the guided antitank missile.

From a hover, targets at a distance of 4,920 to 8,202 feet could be engaged most effectively. Maximum combat range was about 13,000 feet. The missile's accuracy declined notably near the maximum combat range, because when the cruise charge burned out,

the guided antitank missile's speed fell and the control surfaces lost effectiveness. Unguided, the missile could cover a distance of up to 14,763 feet.

Shturm-V (9M114)

The Shturm-V (Штурм-В; NATO: AT-6 Spiral) was developed in the late 1960s to early 1970s as a supersonic, semiautomatically guided, second-generation antitank missile. It was envisaged that land-based, ship-based, and helicopter-fired versions of the guided antitank missile would be placed in service; however, only the Shturm-S for the land forces and the Shturm-V for helicopters were in fact realized. The letter *V* stood for *Vertolyot*, or helicopter.

The Shturm-V was originally envisaged as the Mi-24's main armament system, but development delays made it necessary to use the Falanga guided antitank missile as a stopgap solution.

Between 1972 and 1974, the Shturm-V guided antitank missile was tested as armament for the Mi-24. Several modifications to the guidance system were found necessary, and the updated system was given the designation Raduga-Sha. The earlier analog computer was replaced by a digital one, making the guidance system of the Shturm guided antitank missile complex more capable than the earlier model. It made it possible for the helicopter to take more-aggressive evasive maneuvers sooner after the missile was launched.

On March 28, 1976, the missile was officially placed in service with the Mi-24V attack helicopter.

Until it was fired, the 9M114 Shturm missile was housed in a combined transport-and-launch container. The tube-shaped container could be made of aluminum or plastic and protected the missile from damage and the elements. It was attached to the launch rail by using quick-fit fasteners and could be loaded in a short time. The missile was launched through the cover of the launch tube.

The missile with container weighed 102 pounds, and without the container it tipped the scales at 69 pounds. Its length was 45.8 inches, and it had a caliber of 5 inches. The deployed stabilizing fins spanned 18.4 inches. In transport configuration they were folded, exactly like the control fins. Not until the missile was launched did they deploy and give the missile its stabilizing spin in flight.

The missile consisted of the warhead, which included the hollow charge, fuse, piezoelectric element, and a safety; the guidance cell, with the supply

Shturm-V guided antitank missile containers on an Mi-24P. *Normann*

installations for power and gas plus the control system, including actuators; the engine cell, with launch and cruise engines; and the equipment cell, which housed the radio receiver equipment and the infrared source. An additional accelerator engine was used to launch the missile from the container, which after the missile was ejected fell to the ground.

After leaving the container, the missile's launch engine ignited and accelerated it to 1,738 to 8,137 feet per second within two seconds. The cruise engine then took over, maintaining the missile's velocity for a further five seconds. After burnout the missile continued flying because of its great kinetic energy, slowly losing speed. Maximum velocity over maximum launch range was on average 1,312 feet per second and was thus clearly in the supersonic range.

The missile's dead zone was 1,300 feet in size, and maximum range was listed as 16,400 feet (3.1 miles). Operational experience showed that it was entirely possible to accurately strike a target at maximum range. Deviation from the aiming point at that range was about 19 to 23 inches. At distances of 11,500 to 13,000 feet, however, it proved difficult to distinguish between friend and foe.

As already described, the missile was guided semiautomatically. The operator kept the target in the reticle of his sighting mechanism, and an infrared direction finder measured the discrepancy between the missile's position and the sight line, from which a digital computer produced the corresponding guidance commands and transmitted them to the rocket by means of a radio command unit. A laser rangefinder monitored distance to the target. The range values were used to determine the missile's flight profile. When fired at a close-range target, the missile was steered onto the sight line as soon as possible to ensure a precise hit. When launched at a target farther away, the missile was initially guided 10 to 16 feet above the sight line. This prevented the operator's view of the target from being disrupted, while simultaneously preventing the missile from striking the ground or other obstacles. Not until the missile was approaching the target was it automatically guided to the sight line in order to strike the target precisely.

The effectiveness of the warhead was dependent on speed and range. If the missile struck the target perpendicularly, it was capable of penetrating about 23 to 25 inches of monolithic armor plate. As a rule, this was not sufficient to penetrate the frontal armor of a modern battle tank, which is why the follow-up Ataka-V was developed. The model 9M114M, with the ability to penetrate 28 to 31 inches of monolithic armor plate, was developed as a stopgap solution and used in the mid-1980s.

This Kazakh Mi-24P is launching a Shturm guided antitank missile. The launch engine has already burned out and has been left behind. The helicopter is also dispensing flares. *Rostvertol PLC*

In 1981, the 9M114F version was created for use in Afghanistan. In principle it was identical to the guided antitank missile, but it had a fuel-air warhead for engaging soft and living targets.

Ataka-V (9M120)

The Ataka-V (9M120) guided antitank missile (Атака-В; NATO designation AT-9 Spiral-2) was a direct development of the Shturm-V (9M114), described in the previous section. Like it, it was a helicopter-fired, supersonic, second-generation, semi-automatically controlled, guided antitank missile, whose command transmission was by radio. The Ataka-V was developed by the KMB design bureau based in the city of Kolomna in the early 1980s, when it became obvious that then-current Soviet guided antitank missiles would most probably have difficulty penetrating the frontal armor of the next generation of NATO battle tanks then about to enter service.

The design of the Shturm-V offered sufficient growth potential to create a modern, sufficiently capable guided weapon with which to engage heavily armored vehicles as well as slower, low-flying aerial targets. It was therefore possible to bring the missile to full operational readiness in a relatively short time.

Development work began at the beginning of the 1980s, and the first Ataka-V missiles entered service with the Soviet military in 1986.

The Ataka-V was carried in a combined transport-and-launch container and could be attached to the corresponding stations on an attack helicopter quickly and simply by using quick-fit fasteners.

The general design of the Ataka-V was in principle identical to that of the Shturm-V, but it featured more-modern and clearly more-capable electronics, giving the missile greater accuracy than its predecessor. Targets could be hit with a probability of 95 percent under optimal conditions, while under adverse conditions the chance of a hit was about 65 percent. The improved electronics made it possible to more accurately control the final phase of the flight to the target, so that under favorable conditions it was possible to strike the thinner top armor of an enemy tank. The advances in microelectronics made in the 1980s gave the missile improved resistance to jamming.

The weapon's range was also improved, initially to 19,700 feet (3.7 miles), through use of a longer-lasting cruise engine. On subsequent versions, range was further increased to 10 miles (experimental models even reached distances of 10 miles, and it was found that accuracy at such distances was less dependent on the abilities of the missile than the quality of the optical devices needed to guide the weapon).

The most important innovation was the creation of an improved warhead. It was designed as a tandem hollow charge and was therefore capable of also engaging vehicles equipped with reactive armor. The

Ataka-V guided antitank missile on display at an aviation trade fair. *Rostvertol PLC*

146

This modern Russian Mi-35M is equipped with an eightfold launcher for Ataka-V and Shturm-V guided antitank missiles. *Micheyev via Rostvertol PLC*

first warhead variants were capable of penetrating 31.5 to 33.5 inches of monolithic steel armor plate after passing through reactive armor. Under the same conditions a further developed warhead penetrated up to 37 inches of armor steel.

A guided-missile variant with a fuel-air warhead was developed for use against soft targets, and a version with an expanding rod warhead and proximity fuse was adopted for use against helicopters.

9M120	Tandem hollow charge with penetrative ability of up to 33 inches; range 19,685 ft.
9M120M	Tandem hollow charge with penetrative ability of up to 37 inches; range 26,246 ft.
9M120F	Fuel-air warhead; range 19,685 ft.
9M120O	Expanding-rod warhead and proximity fuse for engaging aerial targets; range 22,965 ft.

Air-to-Air Missiles

The Mi-24 was originally not envisaged for the use of air-to-air missiles. When the Americans began experimenting with air-to-air missiles mounted on their helicopters, the Soviet Union began similar experiments with these weapons.

They first attempted to add the Strela-2M portable surface-to-air missile to the Mi-24V's armament. The Strela-2M was housed in a combined transport-and-launch container just like the Shturm guided antitank missile. Mounts were produced for these containers, and the weapons were attached with quick-fit fasteners.

Tests revealed that it was possible to use the Strela-2M, but since the missile's range seemed inadequate there was no large-scale introduction of the modification.

Later, when the Igla missile became available, the option of installing the weapon on the Mi-24 was taken up again. The arming of Mi-24s with the Igla never really took place on a large scale, probably because the more modern Ataka-V and Shturm-V guided antitank missiles were also capable of engaging enemy helicopters, and at distances beyond the range of the Igla.

During the Cold War, some Mi-24s were fitted with launch rails for R-60 (NATO code name Aphid) air-to-air missiles. Launch rails were installed on the inner stub wing pylons. Helicopters so armed were supposed to operate near the border and, if necessary, intercept violators of Soviet airspace. During combat exercises by the 16th Air Army of the GSSD (Group of Soviet Forces in Germany), it was found that under normal climatic conditions for central Europe, the R-60M missile could detect another helicopter or propeller-driven aircraft only up to a range of 2,000 feet.

There are photos on the internet of R-60 missiles on the launch rails for the Falanga guided antitank missile; however, these do not reflect operational reality, but rather they must be seen as a joke by the ground crews.

Personal Weapons

In addition to the weapons systems included in the design of the Mi-24, there were additional weapons on the attack helicopters that were used by the crew for self-defense or carried by the troops flying in the helicopter. During the Afghanistan war it was standard to equip the flight engineer with a heavy machine gun so that he could open fire on targets that appeared on the side.

Makarov Pistol

The Makarov pistol was an automatic pistol with a caliber of 9.2 × 18 mm. Its design was closely related to that of the Walther PP developed in Zella-Mehlis. The Walther PP design documents were taken as war booty to the Soviet Union, where the designer Makarov used them to adapt the weapon to take the newly developed 9.2 × 18 mm standard cartridge.

In 1951, the Makarov pistol became the standard Soviet pistol and as such was always carried by helicopter pilots as their personal weapon. The Makarov was a weapon with small dimensions, low weight, and simple construction. It was robust and reliable, at least as long as one did not bend the tension spring through excessive cleaning. The pistol's accuracy left something to be desired, however, and its range was limited, which is why it was supplemented or replaced by the AKSU-74 (AKS-74U) assault rifle during the war in Afghanistan.

Kalashnikov AK-47 and AK-74 Family

From the beginning, the Mi-24 helicopter was intended to transport soldiers into battle. The cargo compartment windows could be opened so that they could employ their weapons during flight. There was an extraction mechanism above each window to get rid of the powder gas created when the assault rifle was fired. A flexible hose was attached to it, with an adapter at the end that fit onto the case cover of a Kalashnikov. Powder gas, which exited when the gun was reloaded, was sucked out and vented outside, thus reducing the amount of carbon dioxide in the freight compartment during firing.

The name Kalashnikov has become a synonym for the legendary assault rifle family. It includes assault rifles with calibers of 7.62×39 mm and 5.45×39 mm and with fixed stocks or folding stock / shoulder rest, light machine guns, and short versions of the weapon.

All Kalashnikovs were gas operated with a rotary bolt mechanism, and they distinguished themselves through their extremely robust design and absolute reliability under all conceivable conditions. The variants differed mainly in barrel length. All other components were interchangeable.

The AKS-74U short version was carried as a personal weapon by many pilots in Afghanistan. As a rule, the canteen and emergency rations were removed from the forced-landing packet to make room for the weapon in the Mi-24's cramped cockpit. Their place was taken by the weapon and a spare magazine. Many pilots also carried an F-1 hand grenade as the weapon of last choice. Since experience had shown how the enemy treated his prisoners, many pilots thought it better to blow themselves up in the air than to allow themselves to be captured by the *dushmani*.

Kalashnikov PK Machine Gun

In the war in Afghanistan, the *dushmani* very quickly learned never to get into a frontal duel with an Mi-24. Instead they trusted in their excellent camouflage, let the helicopters fly by, and then shot at them from the side, aiming for the unarmored side cockpit glazing.

To counter this threat, the flight engineers who always flew into action with the Mi-24s were equipped with a Pulemet Kalashnikov (PK) heavy machine gun. His task was to scan the terrain to the sides of the helicopter and if the enemy appeared to open fire on him.

The PK was the standard heavy machine gun of the Soviet military and its allies. It was used as a portable weapon for field use (PK), in all armored vehicles as a pistonless coaxial machine gun (PKT), and also a as fixed forward-firing armament in the Mi-2 helicopter.

The PK machine gun was a gas-operated weapon and had a gas piston and a rotary bolt mechanism. In contrast to the AK-47 assault rifle, the gas cylinder was mounted under the barrel instead of over it. This was necessary to ensure easy access to the weapon's barrel.

Like the Kalashnikov assault rifles, the PK also stood out because of its robust design and outstanding reliability. It was almost trouble free. Due to its high rate of fire, like all machine guns it tended to fire hot after long bursts. It was therefore designed to have interchangeable barrels. The barrel could be removed with two simple hand movements, and a replacement barrel could then be fitted. To prevent the gunner from burning his hands, the barrel was equipped with a wood-covered carry handle.

PK machine guns are belt fed, using nondisintegrating metal belts. The ammunition used is the $7.62 \times 54R$ design, which has its origins in the days of the czars.

Soviet AK-47

PKM heavy machine gun. *Wiki*

Self-Defense Systems

Radar-Warning Devices

The SPO-10 Sirena-3M (Сирена-3M) radar-warning receiver was used in the Mi-24D. The SPO-10 (станция предупреждения об облучении) was able to detect enemy radars at distances of 28 to 31 miles.

The device was equipped with four antennas mounted on the helicopter's stub wings. The antennas were oriented so that each monitored electronic transmissions from one quadrant around the helicopter. The individual antenna channels were fed into the SPO-10, and a potential threat was displayed on an indicator in the cockpit.

The indicator consisted of a round housing on which a stylized aircraft was depicted. In the housing were four lamps, each symbolizing one quadrant. For night use it was possible to dim the lamps to avoid blinding the pilot.

If the warning device received a radar signal, the pilot received an optical indication in which one or more of the warning device's lamps illuminated and an acoustic signal also sounded. A radar operating in search mode produced in the SPO-10 a rhythmic illumination of the lamps and the simultaneous sounding of the warning signal. Since each illumination of the helicopter by a search radar generated its own warning, the changes in the radar's search behavior could be represented visually and acoustically. The tighter the radar focused its scanning beam, the more frequently the helicopter was illuminated and the faster the lamps blinked, with a faster series of warning signals. If a fire control beam locked onto the helicopter, a continuous more urgent tone sounded and the warning lamps indicating the direction of the threat remained lit.

The Mi-24V and subsequent versions used the improved SPO-15 Beryosa system. It indicated the direction of the radar illumination with large, easily recognizable lamps much more precisely than could the SPO-10, and also determined if the radar emissions came from above or below. A semicircle of small

The SPO-10 radar-warning device's indicator. *Normann*

The SPO-15's indicator box in a Cyprian Mi-35P. *Rostvertol*

lights also displayed the direction of other secondary radar emissions.

There was a ring-shaped indicator that displayed information about the strength of the received radar emissions. Another series of indicator lamps defined the type of radar that was illuminating the helicopter. The system provided warnings for air-intercept radars; long-, medium-, and short-range antiaircraft missile complexes; search radars; and AWACS systems.

ASO-2V Flare Dispenser

All Mi-24s built early in the type's production life left the factory without flare dispensers. The military did not think such a system necessary, since it was assumed that enemy fighters equipped with infrared-guided air-to-air missiles would hardly be in a position to engage in a duel with helicopters flying just above the surface of the earth. The appearance of man-portable surface-to-air missiles was acknowledged; however, no countermeasures were taken. This changed when the war in Afghanistan began.

Combat experience there showed that the man-portable surface-to-air missile posed a growing threat to helicopters and aircraft. Henceforth, all Mi-24 attack helicopters were fitted with ASO-2V flare dispensers. Containers for the replaceable flare dispensers were attached to the helicopter's tail boom by using tension bands. At first there were two flare dispensers; later, four were mounted.

Two dispensers (thirty-two flares each) aimed to port, the other two to starboard. This enabled flares to be fired to either side, depending on which direction the threat came from.

Two control elements for the flare dispensers were installed in the gunner's cockpit. The main control panel made it possible for the gunner to select the size of the flare salvo. Series of four to sixteen flares could be selected. It was also possible to select the interval between releases. In rapid-fire mode, a flare was launched every two seconds, while in slow-fire mode the interval was six seconds. The firing of individual flares was also possible from the main control panel.

Because the main control panel was poorly placed ergonomically, there was an easy-to-reach secondary panel that allowed the gunner to select the flares' direction of fire. Of course, it also had a firing button for release of the countermeasures.

The ASO-2V fired LO-56 and later PPI-26-1V flares for use against missiles with infrared seeker heads. Tests showed that the LO-56 was less effective. The temperature and burn duration of the LO-56 were too low, and they were capable of decoying only 10 to 15 percent of infrared-guided missiles. It was therefore replaced by the PPI-26-1V.

Experience in Afghanistan showed that if used properly, with the new flares the system was capable of reliably diverting even the most modern surface-to-air missiles, such as the American Stinger. The protection provided by the ASO-2V, if used properly, was almost 90 percent. For the system to work, in the presence of Stinger missiles it was necessary to have flares in the air at all times. At heights less than 4,900 feet above the ground, it was therefore necessary to continuously launch flares at two-second intervals. At altitudes greater than 4,900 feet, the flares were launched at six-second intervals.

To minimize the use of flares, in Afghanistan long-distance flights were made at altitudes of 10,000 feet or more, because the Stinger could not reach those heights. The use of flares was important during attacks and withdrawals. The flare dispensers were supposed to be activated seven to ten seconds before reaching the effective range of the surface-to-air missiles. During this phase of the mission, flares were launched continuously at intervals of two seconds. According to the manual, use of the ASO-2V was supposed to continue after an attack until the helicopter reached a distance of 10,000 feet from the target, or until it was seven to ten seconds beyond the surface-to-air missile's effective range.

While older versions of the Mi-24 were retrofitted with the ASO-2V, flare dispensers were installed on new helicopters at the factory. These were mounted on either side of the fuselage and held three packages, each of thirty-two flares, per side.

Some Mi-35M helicopters carry the modern Vitebsk flare dispenser system.

Infrared Jammers

The SOEP-V1A (СОЭП-В1А) infrared jammer, alias L166V Ispanka (NATO code name Hot Brick), consists of an infrared emitter (xenon lamp) mounted on the fuselage spine of the Mi-24, and a control panel in the gunner's cockpit. It protects the helicopter against missiles with infrared seeker heads by transmitting amplitude-modulated light disturbances, which are supposed to limit a missile seeker head's ability to accurately acquire its target. The protection generated by Ispanka covers an area of from one to eleven o'clock (30 to 330 degrees) in the horizontal plane and an area of −30 to +10 degrees in the vertical. All-around protection is not possible with Ispanka, since the fuselage blocks the jamming beam in the direction of flight. The system is most effective from two to five o'clock and from seven to ten o'clock. In that zone, an approaching infrared missile is diverted with a probability of up to 80 percent. The Ispanka is less effective directly to the rear (20%–60%).

Direct sunlight from the direction of the incoming rocket limits Ispanka's effectiveness considerably.

The Ispanka infrared system consists of a heat device that, after a five-minute warm-up phase, can operate for two hours in continuous mode and after use must be cooled down for an hour. Conical mirrors are placed above and below the heat generator. Around

the whole thing are two so-called modulation grids, which are thin-walled cylinders with slots. One grid is fixed, while the second rotates around the fixed grid. The rotation speed determines the transmitted impulse frequency. It can be changed by ground personnel so that the search frequency matches that of different infrared seeker heads.

The device's outer surface consists of a layer of ceramic that allows only light in the infrared spectrum to pass through, while that visible to the human eye is blocked.

Ispanka can be fitted with a metal cover to protect the system from damage and dirt.

The L166V system intended for export has the designation Ispanka (Испанка). The systems used by the Soviet military are called Lipa (липа), which is an abbreviation for the Russian technical term for infrared jammer lamp (Лампа инфракрасная помех). They use a different heating element (nickel-chrome spirals).

AVU Heat Baffle

In the early 1980s, following their initial bad experiences in Afghanistan, the Soviets began looking for a means to improve their helicopters' survivability against man-portable surface-to-air missiles. They came up with the idea of screening the hot exhaust gases from the engines from direct view and mixing them with cool air to lower their temperature. The goal was to reduce the helicopters' infrared signature and make the missiles' seeker heads less effective.

Box-shaped housings were placed in front of the engine exhausts, whose job it was to allow cold air in at the front, mix it with the hot exhaust gases, and then divert the mixture upward into the rotor stream, where it was supposed to be further swirled and cooled. They called the system AVU (ЭВУ: экранно-выхлопных устройств).

The first attempts to build an AVU were not really successful. Analysis by the TsAgi Institute showed that the system's effectiveness was low, and the passage of the rotor blades through the diverted gases produced infrared flashes that magically attracted infrared-guided missiles.

The system was therefore redesigned several times and eventually succeeded in reducing the helicopter's heat signature by about 50 percent. Cooling and swirling of the exhaust gases so distorted the IR signature that a contrast-poor image of the helicopter

Ispanka and flare dispensers on a Cyprian Mi-35P. *Rostvertol PLC*

Early unsuccessful version of the AVU during field trials. *OKB Mil*

was formed in the missile's seeker head. This was good enough to decisively reduce the effectiveness of first-generation man-portable missiles such as the American Redeye or the Soviet Strela-2, especially if the helicopter was also equipped with flare dispensers. The AVU's effectiveness was no longer sufficient against modern missile types, however. The system was tested under operational conditions in Afghanistan in 1982.

This showed that use of the AVU increased fuel consumption by about 6 percent. The added weight and drag also resulted in minor reductions in maximum speed and ceiling. Under extreme high-altitude conditions and at high temperatures, the AVU affected the helicopter's performance so badly that it could not be used. To counter this, the units tried to save weight wherever they could; in some cases they even removed the helicopter's armor. In case of doubt, however, helicopter crews preferred to do away with the AVU.

Despite this, the AVU combined with other defensive measures made an important contribution to the helicopter's survivability. From 1984 onward, therefore, all Mi-24s were built to accommodate the AVU.

This Mi-35M is equipped with the AVU system. *Alexey Micheyev via Rostvertol PLC*

Row of section
combat formation

In Combat

Mi-24 Tactics in Europe

The Mi-24 was developed for a potential military conflict in the heart of Europe. It was designed for the role of flying armored personnel carrier, using the same tactics that had been used by the Il-2 *Sturmovik* during the Second World War. The following information is based on the tactical thoughts of the National People's Army (NVA) of the German Democratic Republic, which were essentially similar to Soviet ideas, and how they were presented in service regulations for operational use by the Mi-24 crews and the army air forces.

After the introduction of the helicopter into service, the initial question concerned which branch of the service it should belong to. Should, as before, only the air forces have the right to support friendly troops from the air, or should the land forces be given their own flying units? The debate was protracted, but ultimately the view became more widespread that the attack helicopter should be allocated to the land forces. The result was the creation of the army air forces in the 1980s.

In the NVA, and of course the Soviet military as well, the army air forces were seen as the basic means for supporting one's own troops. They were envisaged primarily for combating enemy forces at and near the front. New roles were defense against enemy helicopters, reconnaissance, and the laying of minefields.

On the basis of these fundamental concepts, the Mi-24 was supposed to carry out a variety of tasks, the most important of which was the destruction of enemy targets located in or just behind the front lines. The Mi-24 was also supposed to be employed to oppose air or sea landings by the enemy and to engage both the air and sea transport used by the enemy, and also to destroy enemy forces that had already landed.

In keeping with the military thinking of the NVA, attack helicopters were also to land troops in the enemy's rear and protect and support airborne landing operations.

CHAPTER 6

The search, rescue, and recovery of pilots in distress formed part of the operational spectrum of Mi-24 crews, as did the landing and recovery of reconnaissance units and special forces.

Secondary tasks included aerial reconnaissance, fire direction in support of the artillery, the laying of mines from the air, transport missions in support of friendly forces, and the evacuation of the wounded and the sick from the combat zone.

The true mission of the Mi-24 crews was to engage the enemy at the forward edge and at tactical depth in the combat zone.

Attack Procedures

Four methods were envisaged for use in combat: engaging the enemy from the hover, from forward flight, from a dive, and from a pull-up.

The **attack from a hover** was regarded by the NVA as the primary method for defending against an enemy armored thrust. Ambush positions occupied by one or two Mi-24s were to be set up in the enemy's direction of action. These positions were to be set up behind masking terrain formations, forests, or towns. Each ambush position had to include a flight control officer, who observed the enemy's approach and coordinated the subsequent engagement.

The Mi-24s took off on the flight control officer's order, acquired their assigned targets, and engaged them with guided antitank missiles from maximum combat range. After opening fire, the Mi-24s left their initial firing positions and moved to secondary positions from which to undertake follow-up attacks on the enemy tanks. They could, however, also circle at very low level in a readiness zone and wait for the flight control officer's order to attack again.

Attacking from a hover in ambush positions made it possible for Mi-24s to employ their weaponry under almost ideal conditions with respect to firing range and target assignment, to avoid enemy antiaircraft weapons, and to exploit the element of surprise.

A disadvantage was that the Mi-24 vibrated more heavily in a hover than in forward flight, reducing the accuracy and thus the likelihood of a hit by the guided antitank missile. The guided antitank missile was the only practical weapon for engaging armored vehicles from a hover; unguided rockets and cannon were not powerful enough to be used with success against armored vehicles in such a position. Bombs, napalm canisters, and cluster weapons could of course not be used from a hover without endangering the Mi-24 itself.

The **attack from horizontal flight** was the main attack method used by the Mi-24. It enabled all the armaments carried by the helicopter to be employed successfully. The approach to the target had to be made in extreme low-level flight to avoid early detection by the enemy. Upon reaching effective weapons range, the Mi-24 was to climb to attack height and strike identified targets with guided antitank missiles. After releasing its weapons, the Mi-24 was supposed to turn away if the enemy was protected by antiaircraft defenses, or if this was not the case, to continue attacking the enemy aggressively with rockets, bombs, and guns.

The advantage of the attack from horizontal flight lay in its concealed approach to the target and the associated favorable conditions for overcoming the enemy's air defenses. The disadvantage was that the helicopter's low approach height meant that targets were acquired well inside the maximum effective range of the guided antitank missiles, and the use of multiple guided antitank missiles before reaching the effective range of the enemy's air defenses was not possible. The firing of unguided rockets at armored targets also had little effect. As a rule, rockets were not sufficiently powerful to penetrate the frontal armor of modern battle tanks.

The **attack from a dive** was therefore preferred for the use of unguided rockets. After approaching the target, which had to be done at extreme low level, the Mi-24 climbed to attack height and, after spotting and identifying the target, dove on the enemy. This enabled targets behind cover to be placed under fire. Another advantage was that this attack method enabled the helicopters to fire at the thinner top armor of enemy tanks, which significantly increased the chance of destroying them.

The attack from a dive also had several disadvantages. For one, the helicopter exposed itself to the enemy's air defenses, and therefore this method could reasonably be used only if the enemy's antiaircraft

Mi-24s and BMD-2s during a combat exercise. *Russian MoD*

Two Mi-24Ps in formation. *Russian MoD, Balashova*

system was destroyed or disoriented. For another, the usable weapons array was severely limited. For technical reasons, guided antitank missiles could not be used with a good chance of success, and the use of bombs, napalm canisters, and wing-mounted weapons exposed the Mi-24 to enemy fire. The manual stated that the Yak-B machine gun could be used in dives of up to 15 degrees, whereas the revolving turret could be used by the gunner at dive angles up to 10 degrees. The machine gun had to be placed in fixed mode for use at steeper angles. The weapon was then operated by the pilot, who aimed the weapon at vehicles by using his gunsight.

The principal weapon used in diving attacks was the unguided rocket, which achieved its best accuracy and greatest effectiveness by using this attack method.

The last and least usable attack method was the **attack from a pull-up**. This method was suitable only for attacking large-area targets and was carried out with unguided rockets.

It was intended to place large, well-defended areas under fire without exposing the Mi-24 to the enemy's air defenses. The Mi-24 was supposed to approach at the highest possible airspeed and pull up into a climb at an angle determined before the mission. Upon reaching a predetermined position, the unguided rockets were fired and the helicopter immediately began an evasive maneuver to return to extreme low-level flight and turn away from the target.

When attacking from a pull-up, the Mi-24 assumed the role of a flying mortar. Accuracy was minimal, since the weapons system had not been designed for this method of operation and had no aiming mechanism suitable for the indirect firing of unguided rockets.

The method of attacking from a pull-up was described in various service manuals and handbooks, but it was regarded with some skepticism by the pilots of the Mi-24.

Combat Formation

The use of single Mi-24s over the potential central European battlefield was envisaged only in exceptional cases. Operations by single Mi-24s were conceived as being practical only during special missions.

The smallest tactical unit was the pair, consisting of two Mi-24s. In command was the pilot of the first helicopter, called the pair leader or leader. The number two in the formation was called the led. Two pairs formed a section, which was commanded by a section leader.

Three or four sections formed a squadron, and several squadrons a wing, or in Soviet parlance, a regiment.

The wing was directly attached to the commander of a military district or an army. He was free to use it as he wished.

The battle arrays used by the Mi-24 units varied widely. They operated both in closed formation, which meant that the maximum distance between aircraft was twice the rotor diameter, and open formation.

The closed formation was relatively rarely used, since it required a high degree of attentiveness on the part of the pilot to avoid collisions in the air. This naturally detracted from observation of the battlefield and hindered the accomplishment of his mission. The closed formation was therefore envisaged only if the goal was to penetrate an enemy air defense zone as quickly as possible in a tight and compact formation, or to attack small enemy targets with as many helicopters as possible, or if troops were to be landed in small sectors of terrain.

While flying in open battle array, the distance between the individual Mi-24s was more than two main rotor diameters. Maximum distance was limited by visibility, since the helicopters were supposed to provide each other with mutual support and had to be able to see the pilots of the other helicopters.

Open formations permitted the maximum exploitation of the Mi-24's maneuverability and offered excellent conditions for optimal target search and the precise use of weapons. At the same time they reduced the risk of a collision between two helicopters in the air and minimized the probability that two or more helicopters might be successfully engaged by a single enemy missile.

If the Mi-24 flew in formations in which the distance between the individual helicopters was so great that it was no longer possible to see one another, it was called a decentralized battle array. This were used during transport and airborne landing operations in difficult weather conditions or at night. During combat missions in poor visibility, successive blows could be delivered against individual enemy targets with decentralized formations. Massed attacks were not possible with decentralized battle arrays.

As previously mentioned, the smallest tactical unit of an Mi-24 unit was the pair. Mi-24 pairs usually flew in the battle arrays front (side by side), column (one behind the other), or row (echeloned).

A Georgian
Mi-24V and an
Mi-24P. *Georgian
Ministry of
Defense*

Mi-24P in winter.
Russian Army

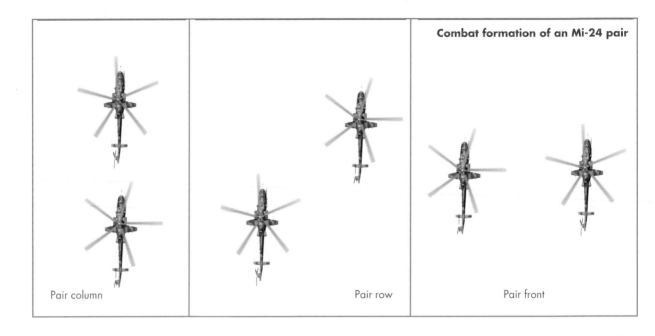

Pair column   Pair row   Pair front

Two pairs formed a section. The four Mi-24s could assume the battle arrays front (side by side), column (one behind the other), column of pairs, row (echeloned), row of pairs, and wedge (finger-four formation).

A squadron, which was formed from several sections, operated in the battle formations column of sections (one behind the other), row of sections (echeloned), front of sections (one beside the other), and snake (sections flying one behind the other, with alternating sections displaced to the side). The battle arrays of the individual sections could vary.

A wing formed itself as a column of squadrons or as a line of squadrons, and once again the battle array within the individual squadrons and sections could differ.

The objective of every battle array was to build formations that offered maximum battlefield observation, safe conduct of fire, and best protection for the Mi-24 crews in any situation.

Since the strategy of the Warsaw Pact was an offensive one until the mid-1980s, the attack was also the main form of engagement for the attack helicopter units. Because they had to expect to meet a powerful, well-organized opponent, the military of the Eastern defense pact assumed that massive blows by attack helicopter units would be necessary to achieve victory on the battlefield.

It was the view of the NVA that massed Mi-24 units had to organize their battle array so that the individual groups could carry out a wide variety of tasks.

It was the task of the main group to carry out the actual combat assignment. It could engage enemy land and sea targets as a strike group, transport weapons and materiel as an air transport group, or lay mines to render an area impassable. As a rule, the majority of the deployed helicopters were part of the main group.

Security groups were detached to support the main group. Their mission was to create favorable conditions for the main group's combat actions.

The security group included the follow-up reconnaissance group, the target-marker group, the electronic warfare group, the group to destroy enemy air defense systems (suppression group), the group to cover the main group against attacks by enemy helicopters and aircraft (cover group), the group to divert and deceive the enemy (demonstration group), and the group to recover and rescue helicopter crews in distress (SAR group).

The task of the **follow-up reconnaissance group** was to gather information about the targets or landing sites, check the weather and route to the target, and conduct post-strike reconnaissance in the target area. It had to fly ahead of the main group so that the

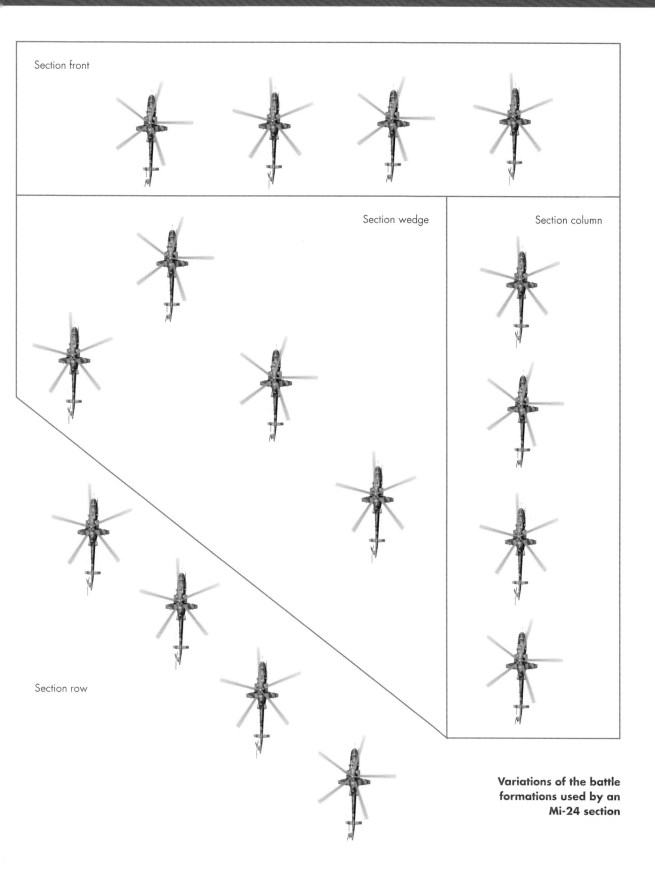

Section front

Section wedge

Section column

Section row

Variations of the battle formations used by an Mi-24 section

gathered information could be passed to the commander of the main group and worked by him into his battle plan.

The **target marker group**'s mission was to obtain more-precise information about the location of targets or landing sites and, if necessary, mark targets or landing sites with radio or visual markers. The group was supposed to act as pathfinders, fly ahead of the main group, guide it to the target, and, if necessary, provide target illumination.

The target marker and follow-up reconnaissance groups were often combined.

The **countermeasures group** was supposed to suppress enemy radar sites of all kinds, as well as antiaircraft artillery fire control stations, and render ineffective the seeker heads of guided surface-to-air missiles. Its position in the overall formation was determined by the commander of the formation, on the basis of local conditions. It should be noted that the NVA had no helicopters with special active jamming systems. Other Warsaw Pact armies, in particular the Soviet Army, had variants of the Mi-8 / Mi-17 helicopters fitted with excellent jamming equipment.

The **suppression group** had to engage the enemy's antiaircraft positions en route to the target and in the target area itself. Enemy antiaircraft positions were either to be destroyed or, if this was not possible, suppressed long enough that they posed no threat to the main group. The suppression group could also be used to provide direct air support during and after the landing of troops. The suppression group or groups operated ahead of and on the flanks of the main group and positioned themselves so that continuous cover was provided against enemy antiaircraft weapons.

The **cover group**'s role was to defend against enemy helicopters and aircraft, destroying enemy helicopters or, by engaging them, occupying them before they could use their weapons systems on the main-group helicopters. The cover group's attack helicopters were supposed to cover the main group in all directions and, in doing so, operate at a distance from the main group that enabled it to intercept aerial threats on a timely basis. This group's helicopter pilots would have received special training in aerial combat.

The **demonstrative or diversion group** had to divert the enemy's air defenses from the main group's direction of action by carrying out mock attacks. Its position in the main group was determined by local conditions.

The **group for rescuing crews in distress** was formed from the assets of the main group, specifically those attack helicopters flying at the rear of the formation. When ordered to do so by the formation leader, they had to rescue crews in distress.

Air Strike

An **air strike against targets at tactical depth** by an Mi-24 unit of course began with **takeoff by the unit** after preparations and the issuing of orders. This unit was supposed to take off under cover and as quickly as possible. To maintain concealment, air traffic control and the helicopters were to limit radio traffic to the extent possible, or the entire takeoff process took place under radio silence. At night, the use of light signals was restricted to the absolute minimum. Time was saved during the unit's takeoff through the use of group takeoffs, reducing departure intervals, and the selection of helicopter dispersals that shortened the required taxi time as much as possible. This was diametrically opposed, however, by the requirement for decentralized parking and camouflaging of the unit on the ground.

The subsequent **assembly of the unit** in the air and moving into battle array were supposed to be carried out at low and very low altitudes. In this way, enemy radars were prevented from detecting the helicopter formation and providing early warning of their approach.

Three different methods were used to form up into battle array as quickly as possible. Takeoffs by individual helicopters and helicopter subunits could be timed so that the required battle array intervals were established on takeoff. The entire unit was thus more or less in battle array from the point of takeoff.

If there was insufficient space for a massed takeoff by the unit, assembly in the air could be accomplished through speed maneuvers. The first aircraft to become airborne initially flew at reduced airspeed, while those that got airborne later tried to catch up by flying at full power. When all aircraft had reached the unit and taken up their positions in the battle array, the entire formation assumed the predetermined cruise speed.

This method had several disadvantages. For one, it took a relatively long time for all the helicopters to take up their positions in the battle formation. Second, there was always the danger that stragglers might not

A squadron in
formation for a
mass takeoff.
Mambour

catch up with the formation or do so only with difficulty. Third, the last Mi-24s to take off used more fuel by flying at high speed, reducing the range of the entire formation considerably.

Therefore, when possible, an attempt was made to form up in the air by circling near the takeoff site or by flying a 180-degree turn.

The unit's flight to the target could be carried out as a single formation or on several different routes. Wings and squadrons could operate on one or more routes, while it was not envisaged that sections and pairs would separate.

The flight on several routes was used if the unit had to split up for different battle assignments in different areas of operation. The use of one flight route took place when the entire unit was sent against a single target. If there were several targets located close together in the target area, the flight followed one route and the battle array subsequently broke up into pairs and sections. The overall formation broke up near the targets, and individual divisions engaged the various targets.

The attack helicopter unit's flight to the action area was supposed to take place at low and very low altitudes. This minimized the probability that the helicopters would be detected by enemy radar and patrolling fighter aircraft.

As long as the formation was flying over friendly territory, the flight was supposed to be carried out via the shortest route and at the highest economical flight altitude, but here too the principle of selecting a route that eliminated the possibility of early detection also prevailed.

Crossing the front line was regarded as a special problem, since it was assumed that the enemy had an extensive and powerful air defense. The front was therefore supposed to be crossed in sectors in which the air defenses could be suppressed by electronic countermeasures or artillery fire.

Crossing of the front line was supposed to take place as quickly as possible. A massed approach in tight formations was supposed to reduce the crossing time and overwhelm the enemy's air defenses. In this way it was hoped to limit losses to an acceptable level.

Navigation to the target was accomplished using the Mi-24's Doppler navigation system. The NVA, however, relied on the tried-and-true method of dead reckoning. Beginning from a prominent orientation point, speeds and headings were maintained to reach the area of activity with certainty. Should the air strike be carried out against objects on the front line or just beyond it, it was also possible for flight control officers to guide the helicopters to the target. There was also the possibility of navigating the helicopter formation to the action area with the help of the air traffic control system, using radio direction finders, ground-based navigation aids, radio beacons, etc.

Achieving the element of surprise was regarded as one of the most important requirements for the successful completion of a combat mission by an Mi-24 unit. The approach to the target was therefore supposed to be made at extremely low altitudes, exploiting the landscape characteristics, the presence of wooded areas or towns, and even the weather conditions. In daylight, attacks were to be made out of the sun when possible, and at night and twilight, from the direction of the dark part of the horizon. Areas with enemy air defenses were to be avoided if possible.

When the approach to the target began, the attack helicopter unit was to regroup its battle array so that the entire group's firepower could be brought to bear. During the attack, individual Mi-24 crews were supposed to concentrate on previously identified targets but also attack new targets as they appeared. It was to be ensured that each crew concentrate on a single target, avoiding the frittering away of assets or having more than one helicopter attack the same target.

The attack was supposed to begin with a fast approach to the target and to enable the Mi-24s to use their weaponry in a targeted fashion. The attacks were to be made primarily from horizontal flight or a dive. Attacks from a hover were possible but were to be avoided during air strikes, since nearly stationary helicopters were easy targets for the enemy's air defenses.

The initial attack was seen as the most important part of the strike. Its goal was to achieve the highest degree of effectiveness and shock and disorient the enemy.

During the air strike, all Mi-24 crews, no matter which tactical group they belonged to, had to be ready—in addition to their other combat assignments—to engage targets that appeared suddenly, such as nonsuppressed antiaircraft assets, or to fight off counterattacks by enemy helicopters. Attacks on unidentified targets in the immediate vicinity of friendly troops were strictly forbidden.

After the mission was completed or after all weapons had been fired, the Mi-24s withdrew from the target area at the lowest possible altitude. The withdrawal was to be made in a direction that separated the helicopters from other units approaching for an attack, and that was least defended by the enemy's air defenses.

The IFF system was to be switched on as the helicopters crossed the front line, transmitting the signal "friendly helicopters here."

During the return flight, the crews were supposed to return to battle formation if possible and to their landing field at the lowest possible altitude. Radio silence was maintained to the degree possible, and radio traffic between the helicopters and the landing field was kept to an absolute minimum.

Upon arrival at the landing field the battle formation was dissolved. The helicopters had to form a landing sequence and main safe distances between aircraft. The prevailing rule was that damaged helicopters and those low on fuel had priority.

The landing by the unit had to take place rapidly and in the order specified for that landing site. It was possible to carry out group landings to speed up the recovery process, to tighten up the landing intervals, and to use every available surface.

During the entire flight home, during the breakup of the formation, and even during the approach to land, the Mi-24 crews had to search the sky for signs of enemy activity. While regulations called for friendly fighters to cover and defend the attack helicopter unit, it was recognized that this would not always be possible.

If no fighter aircraft could be made available for an attack helicopter strike, the mission commander had to arrange for a return flight escort. These could be attack helicopters that were kept in reserve at the landing site. The return escort took off when the operational unit began its return, flew out to meet the returning helicopters, and defended them against attacks from the air. After the operational unit landed, the escort unit's helicopters could also land.

Helicopters that had landed were immediately dispersed, camouflaged, and prepared for the next sortie. Damaged aircraft had to be made ready for action again as quickly as possible. Attack helicopters that were so damaged that they could not be taxied to their dispersals were to be towed away by the ground personnel or, if necessary, camouflaged and repaired on the spot.

Combat against Surface-to-Air Missiles and Enemy Aircraft

Overcoming the enemy's air defenses was regarded as an important precondition for the successful carrying out of combat assignments.

To enable them to overcome enemy air defenses with minimal losses, Mi-24 crews were supposed to employ basic tactical methods, which they practiced and constantly refined. This included using the most-favorable routes that took them around areas with the heaviest air defenses, or flying through areas in which the air defenses were suppressed by countermeasures or friendly fire. The flight was to be made at the most favorable altitude, exploiting terrain, available cover, and favorable weather conditions. During a combat mission, the most favorable battle formation was to be chosen. Recognized antiaircraft positions were supposed to be paralyzed by countermeasures group assets or engaged from maximum combat distance, with the Mi-24s remaining outside the most effective firing range of the enemy's air defense. If the enemy nevertheless opened fire, the pilots were supposed to take evasive action immediately and use the helicopter's own jamming equipment.

If the Mi-24s had to carry out operations within the enemy air defense's effective area, attacking surface-to-air missile sites and antiaircraft gun positions had top priority. The use of fire and countermeasures was supposed to create breakthrough lanes in the enemy's defensive belt, in which antiaircraft defenses were destroyed or suppressed to the degree that no opposition was likely. The attack helicopters had to cross the zone of maximum effectiveness of the enemy air defense at high speed, under the protection of jamming and electronic countermeasures (ECM) provided by the countermeasures group, while making abrupt course changes. If possible, the helicopters were supposed to fly through only the edge of the enemy defense's area of effectiveness and expose themselves to enemy fire for just a brief period.

If the enemy employed surface-to-air missiles, each crew member had the duty to immediately warn all other helicopters. On receipt of this information, the formation leader ordered the unit to immediately carry out evasive maneuvers. Missile-evasive maneuvers included heading, altitude, and speed tactics, which were supposed to prevent the successful engagement of the attack helicopters. These included an immediate descent to extreme low level with simultaneous use

The use of flares is vital for survival in the presence of infrared-guided missiles.
Rostvertol PLC

of countermeasures, and exiting the missiles' zone of lethality while exploiting favorable terrain and other cover. Heading changes were also possible in which the highest-possible angular velocity was achieved, which was intended to make missile guidance difficult or even impossible. Here, too, the use of flares and the simultaneous activation of the infrared jammer were vital for survival.

If the attack helicopter unit came within range of enemy antiaircraft guns, course and altitude maneuvers were initiated immediately. Constant changes in range to the gun position and heading changes by the helicopter reduced the effectiveness of the antiaircraft guns. The use of decoys in the battle against enemy antiaircraft guns was seen as counterproductive.

During battle flights in areas covered by enemy fighter aircraft, attack helicopters were instructed to rely on support from friendly fighters or fighter-bombers. Their task was to neutralize enemy airfields and destroy his command-and-control centers, divert him from the attack helicopters' area of action through diversionary measures, and provide escort for the attack helicopter units.

Attack helicopter units were supposed to adopt a formation that enabled them to carry out evasive maneuvers at any time and allowed the helicopters to provide mutual covering fire.

The timely recognition of enemy fighter aircraft was to be ensured by uninterrupted air observation. Each crew was assigned an area of sky to monitor, for which he was responsible. The sighting of enemy fighter aircraft was to be reported immediately, with unidentified aircraft assumed to be hostile.

During encounters with enemy fighters, the Mi-24 crews were to take measures to prevent an enemy attack or at least reduce its effectiveness. These included increases in airspeed, descent to extreme low level, and dispersal of the battle formations.

If the enemy attacked from the forward hemisphere, the Mi-24 pilots had to follow the order to descend in the direction of the enemy. They were to face the enemy, which was supposed to give the Mi-24 the opportunity to return fire and possibly force the enemy to veer off. Flying at extremely low altitude made it difficult for the enemy fighter to spot the Mi-24, especially if its pilot exploited the terrain. Furthermore, then-modern radars had problems tracking and locking on to helicopters flying just above the ground, making it unlikely that they could employ air-to-air missiles (AAMs). Infrared-guided AAMs of the 1970s and 1980s also had difficulties engaging very low-flying helicopters, especially if the weapons had to be used from above.

If enemy fighter aircraft attacked the Mi-24s from the rear hemisphere, the pilots were instructed to immediately turn into the attacker.

The unit commander was supposed to assign special cover groups to defend against enemy helicopters. They were positioned in the battle array so that they could engage attacking enemy helicopters at any time. The Mi-24s in the cover groups were to vary their speed, heading, and altitude to create the most-favorable conditions with which to counter the attack and destroy the enemy helicopters.

The Mi-24 crews were supposed to engage enemy helicopters in aerial combat at low and extremely low altitudes, using their machine gun and cannon armament, unguided rockets, and guided antitank missiles. R-60 infrared-guided missiles were installed on a few Mi-24s of the GSSD (Group of Soviet Forces in Germany) in the 1980s. Later modifications enabled the Mi-24V and Mi-24P to carry Igla portable surface-to-air missiles. If such missiles had been available, they would undoubtedly have been the weapon of choice for air combat. Observations from the Iran-Iraq War showed that guided antitank missiles could be used against enemy helicopters with success.

In the view of the NVA, success in aerial combat could be ensured by a determined approach to the target, an aggressive surprise attack, or the seizure and maintenance of the initiative in close combat. It was therefore important to be the first to spot the enemy. Observation of the airspace around the formation had the utmost priority. The sighting of enemy helicopters had to be reported to the formation leader immediately. He then had to determine the strength of the enemy formation and the type of helicopter; assess its battle array, altitude, and direction of flight; and determine if there were other enemy helicopters in the area.

After evaluating these factors, the unit commander decided whether he should engage in air combat or not.

If he decided to engage, he had to order one or more cover groups, whose task it was to cover the entire formation, to intercept the enemy. The attack helicopters then had to close rapidly with the enemy helicopters and assume a favorable position from which to attack. The most favorable attack position was from out of the sun or from the rear hemisphere, where the enemy pilot's view was limited.

After assuming a favorable attack position, the Mi-24s had to close with the enemy helicopters, take aim, and initiate their attack.

The attack was the decisive phase of the air engagement. It began with aiming and ended when firing stopped. The attack could take place from below, above, or the same altitude. Machine guns and cannon had to be used from a range that guaranteed destruction of the target.

An attack from the rear hemisphere was regarded as the most effective method for the use of weapons.

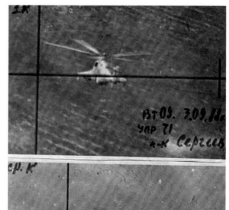

Mi-24V in the sight of another Mi-24 during an air-combat-training sortie. *Payevski via www.16va.be*

After a successful engagement, the Mi-24s were supposed to break off the air battle and return to the formation they were covering. They had to break off the air battle at extremely low altitude, in the direction of the sun or shielding clouds.

If the first attack was not successful, the Mi-24s were supposed to engage in a turning battle and try to achieve a position from which to make another attack.

If was important for the Mi-24s not to pursue a fleeing enemy, since the danger existed that they might be drawn away from the main group. Protection of the main group was the highest priority.

Supporting Friendly Troops in the Area of the Front

One of the attack helicopter's most important tasks was the engagement of objects in the front line and at tactical depth while providing air support for friendly troops. Both the Mi-24 and the Mi-8TB were envisaged for this role, but the latter was intended mainly for use in close proximity to friendly ground forces, while the Mi-24 was to spread out farther and attack enemy objects in the wider surroundings.

The main targets to be engaged (objects) were tanks, armored combat vehicles, armored personnel carriers, and motor vehicles, as well as troops in marching, prebattle, or battle order. Antitank weapons, artillery, and tactical or strategic missiles were also to be attacked while on the move or in firing/launch positions. The destruction of nuclear weapons was of the highest priority.

Radar sites, antiaircraft weapons, and command centers were also targets, as were the enemy's transport, combat, and antitank helicopters.

During air support operations, the battle array of the involved Mi-24 unit could be analogous to that used during an air strike against the enemy's rear and consist of a strike group and several security groups. As usual, these could be post-strike reconnaissance, suppression, and cover groups.

The combat flight was to be carried out at extremely low altitude. Approach to the target was carried out independently, either visually by using the dead reckoning method or by guidance and target assignment by flight control officers on the ground or in other helicopters.

The direction of the approach to the target was to be selected so as to give the helicopters favorable conditions for locating their targets and using their weapons. This was intended to cause the maximum

damage to the target. Care had to be taken to prevent the helicopters from being destroyed by friendly artillery fire. It also had to be ensured that friendly troops were not endangered by the Mi-24s' fire.

The strike group could carry out attacks on a target from one or more directions. During coordinated attacks from different directions, care had to be taken to prevent helicopters from hindering one another's attacks or unintentionally firing on them. During the attack, the Mi-24s were to employ the weapons systems that offered the greatest destructive effect in the target area. To defend against enemy defenses during the attack, in addition to the direct engagement of antiaircraft assets, the pilots were to employ countermeasures and evasive maneuvers against antiaircraft fire and surface-to-air missiles.

If enemy armored units, motorized infantry, and mechanized units were to be encountered fully deployed on the advance, the Mi-24 squadrons were supposed to halt them through a simultaneous strike by all available helicopters or by successive attacks by individual sections and pairs of helicopters.

A pair of Mi-24s lifting off from an ambush position. *Scheffler Collection*

The attack was supposed to take place after the helicopters were summoned from jump-off airfields or ambush positions. In such situations, flight control officers were of vital importance.

The main objective was the destruction of tanks, armored personnel carriers, and other armored vehicles. As a rule of thumb, each Mi-24 squadron was to engage one armored battalion, one motorized infantry, or one infantry battalion. A section operating within a squadron was supposed to engage the enemy in company strength, while individual pairs were to take on armored and motorized infantry platoons.

Attacks against an advancing enemy could be made from a hover at maximum range or be carried out at high speed in level flight or a dive.

Attacks from a hover were supposed to take place from ambush positions only. Pairs and sections were used for such attacks under the command of a flight control officer. To improve accuracy when using guided antitank missiles, after taking off from ambush positions the helicopters could go into forward flight, while ensuring that the guided antitank missiles were used from maximum distance and that the Mi-24s remained beyond the range of the enemy's air defense weapons.

After the attack was made, the attack helicopters had to withdraw, immediately reduce altitude, and seek out another position. They were never supposed to fire twice from the same position. Additional attacks on the enemy were always made from another direction.

If the enemy was in dug-in defensive positions, the Mi-24 squadrons were supposed to attack them in a massive strike, using all their assets, or in successive strikes by individual pairs and sections. Tanks and armored personnel carriers were also important targets here, but antiaircraft and antitank weapons were of equal importance.

Guided missiles and unguided rockets were used to engage the targets, as were machine guns and cannon. As a rule, one squadron would undertake the attack on a company strongpoint, while a section was to engage a platoon strongpoint.

During attacks on fortified enemy positions, it was important to achieve surprise. The approach was to be made as quickly as possible and directly from one's own area. An approach in the lethal zone of the enemy's air defenses was to be avoided. The attack was to be ended, at the latest, when the helicopters were about to enter the effective range of the enemy's antiaircraft machine guns and small arms.

If the enemy units were in marching formation and still in their own rear, Mi-24 units could be sent on forays to seek out and destroy the columns. Since these strikes were associated with penetrations into the tactical depth of enemy territory, they could be carried out only if the enemy's air defenses in the area of the front to be overflown were suppressed or disoriented, or if the Mi-24s were able to create gaps in the enemy's battle array.

Forays were supposed to be carried out only by entire squadrons, with the squadron, as usual, organized into groups with different tactical responsibilities.

Unguided rockets, machine guns, cannon, napalm canisters, bombs, and cluster bombs were supposed to be used to destroy missiles and artillery, command centers, radar sites, and helicopters on their landing fields. Guided antitank missiles would be used to engage tactical and tactical-strategic missiles, which were regarded as potential carriers of nuclear weapons.

Missile launch sites with missiles present, self-propelled artillery, fire-control systems, antenna arrays, and helicopters were considered important individual targets.

If the enemy's location or route of advance was not known, pairs and sections were supposed to be committed in open formation. Their task was to seek out the enemy. This mode of operation, also called free hunting, could cover a certain previously designated area or follow roads. Targets were supposed to be attacked and destroyed as soon as they were discovered. During free-hunting missions the formation leader had great freedom of action when it came to search methods and the carrying out of attacks.

Attack Helicopters Defending against Airborne Landings by the Enemy

On the basis of experience from the Vietnam War, the NVA assumed that if war broke out in the heart of Europe, the Americans, taking advantage of their powerful helicopter units, would employ air-mobile forces. It envisaged large-scale airborne landings in which NATO helicopters would land powerful units deep in the eastern coalition's rear. The enemy's air transport units would obviously be accompanied by attack helicopters.

To defend against such operations, Mi-24 attack helicopters were supposed to work closely with troops of the land forces and frontal aviation forces. The

Mi-24 squadrons were to launch simultaneous full-strength strikes or successive attacks by individual sections and pairs as requested by the land forces.

The most-important targets in the destruction of the enemy's airborne forces were all helicopters on the ground and in the air, air defense assets, artillery, and personnel. Unguided rockets, machine gun and cannon fire, bombs, cluster bombs and napalm canisters, and guided antitank missiles for high-value targets were to be used in their destruction.

To destroy enemy troops in the drop zone, it was necessary to organize the attack helicopters' battle array into strike group, post-strike reconnaissance group, suppression group, and cover group.

When the enemy appeared, the strike group was to split up in the air, with one part taking on the enemy attack helicopters and the other the transport helicopters. If the enemy had already landed, the strike group was to destroy him through repeated attacks from several directions.

The post-strike reconnaissance group was supposed to be the first to enter the area of penetration, identify targets, and assess the situation. The suppression group, which followed the post-strike reconnaissance group, was to immediately engage the enemy's air defense assets and destroy them by the time the strike group arrived. The cover group's attack helicopters were to engage enemy attack helicopters in the air, destroy them, and provide air cover for the strike group in the withdrawal area.

To support friendly ground forces defending against the airborne landing, it was envisaged that transport helicopters would fly in airborne forces, essentially carrying out a counterlanding. The transport helicopters would be covered by Mi-24 attack helicopters. After the airborne forces had been dropped off, both the Mi-24 escort helicopters and the Mi-8TB transport helicopters would take up the battle against the enemy's airborne forces.

Attack Helicopters Defending against Naval Landings by the Enemy

Enemy seaborne invasion troops were supposed to be engaged by attack helicopters in the landing zones in close cooperation with other units of the land, sea, and air forces tasked with coastal defense.

Priority targets were landing vessels and craft, helicopters, tanks, armored fighting vehicles and armored personnel carriers landed by the enemy, and established strongpoints, artillery, and personnel in the coastal sector.

Combating Enemy Special Forces in Rear Areas

Enemy reconnaissance or special forces that had advanced into friendly rear areas were to be engaged by individual attack helicopters operating at low level. If an enemy force was found, the attack helicopter's crew immediately sent a corresponding report to the command center and waited for orders.

If the command center ordered the destruction of the group, it was to be attacked and taken out with unguided rockets and machine gun and cannon fire.

If the capture of the group was ordered, the Mi-24 crew had to keep the intruders under constant observation and if necessary engage them to pin them down and prevent them from escaping. The ultimate goal was their capture by friendly ground forces.

Landing of Friendly Airborne Troops

An Mi-24 was capable of transporting up to eight airborne troops. This was seldomly practiced, however, and was not really popular among Mi-24 crews. Among themselves, Mi-24 crews said that they preferred to transport freight because "freight doesn't grumble, and freight doesn't puke!" The added weight in the Mi-24's cargo compartment also significantly limited its combat characteristics.

Transport helicopters (Mi-8, Mi-17) were therefore the preferred choice for transporting troops during an airborne landing operation, which in turn were protected by Mi-24s.

Smaller airborne operations (tactical airborne landings) were envisaged up to a depth of 30 miles. Large-scale strategic-tactical airborne landings could be carried out up to 60 miles deep into the enemy rear. Starting points for such operations were supposed to be located 31 to 43 or 60 to 75 miles from the front line, which meant that the helicopters had to cover distances of 60 to 120 miles.

While the transport attack helicopter forms the air transport group, the Mi-24 is used in tactical roles by all other groups.

These include the post-strike reconnaissance group, the suppression group, and cover groups to defend against attacks by enemy attack helicopters.

To seize the landing zones and secure the landing by the airborne forces, it was possible to form an advance group consisting of combat and transport helicopters. Upon reaching the landing zones, the advance group was supposed to pin down or destroy the enemy, drop off the airborne troops, and immediately take off again and provide fire support for the seizure of the landing zones. When the main group arrived, the advance group had to cover it against any attacks by the enemy.

To protect the airborne landing group en route to the landing zones, the Mi-24s of the security groups had to destroy the enemy's antiaircraft assets in the area of the front that it would pass over. Enemy air defenses in the landing zone were likewise to be engaged, as were ground forces defending the landing zone. Priority targets included tanks and armored vehicles, artillery and rocket launch sites, and enemy personnel. Relieving enemy units were to be destroyed with all means available.

Attacks on the transport helicopters by enemy helicopters were to be repulsed without being drawn away from the airborne landing group.

Attack Helicopters during the Landing and Recovery of Reconnaissance and Special Forces

The use of scouts and special units in the enemy's rear has a long tradition in the military. With the advent of the helicopter, for the first time there was a weapons system that could drop members of special units deep in enemy territory quickly and also pick them up again.

Because of its freight compartment, which was suitable for transporting personnel, and its ability to shoot its way out in an emergency, the Mi-24 was predestined for this role.

The landing of scouts and special forces in the enemy rear was, as a rule, carried out by single helicopters at night. Missions of this type could also be carried out by day in bad weather.

During preparations for a mission, important measures were taken to prevent discovery by the

enemy. Routes and the landing zone had to be selected to avoid enemy troops and air defenses. This required that the enemy's position be known. Landing sites in the enemy's rear were supposed to be level areas of terrain unoccupied by enemy troops.

A patrol is picked up by an Mi-24. This photo was taken during a demonstration for state and party leaders of the GDR. *Air Force Museum, Gatow*

Because a flight at night or bad weather deep into enemy territory placed high demands on the aircrew, only the best-trained crews were chosen for such missions. The crews also had to be familiar with the terrain over which the mission would be flown, be well informed about the procedures to be used to get past the enemy's air defenses, and be capable of landing even in the most-difficult conditions on small, unmarked landing sites.

Prior to takeoff, the crew was given the latest reconnaissance results regarding the weather, enemy dispositions, and so on. The flight over enemy territory was to be made at extreme low level, with maximum exploitation of the terrain features. Of course, radio slice would be maintained and navigation lights turned off. Landing at the chosen site had to take place under shielded lighting conditions. Landing lights were used only very briefly or, at best, not at all.

During recovery of the scout group, the helicopter crew had to verify the identity of those being picked up. They were to ensure they received the correct password and to receive the signal for "friendly troops here" from those being picked up.

During the rendezvous at the landing site, the crew of the Mi-24 had to establish radio contact with the scouts or, if they had no radio equipment, to search for the location of the group and the landing site by using light signals.

Laying of Minefields from the Air

The laying of minefields from the air was regarded as an emergency measure. It was supposed to be used if the enemy had broken through or had created a breach in the front with nuclear weapons. The laying of mines by attack helicopters was supposed to inflict casualties on the advancing enemy, delay a breakthrough by armored or mechanized infantry, and channel it in a specified direction or stop it.

The attack helicopters could operate separately or act in conjunction with blocking battalions, combat engineers, or regular troops of the land forces.

In addition to the actual mine-laying group, the battle array of an Mi-24 squadron during aerial mine laying was to include a post-strike reconnaissance group, a group to mark the sectors to be mined, and a covering group.

The laying of mines from the air was to be carried out in pairs or sections. It was imperative that the speed and height specified for the type of mine to be dropped be maintained in order to achieve the desired saturation on the ground.

While special mine-laying systems existed for the Mi-8 / Mi-17, Mi-24 units could reach back only on cluster weapon systems such as the KGMU-2 for mining sections of terrain. A stopgap solution was to simply drop mines from the windows of the helicopters.

The sector to be mined was to be approached visually and, if required, marked by ground troops or helicopters of the security group.

In keeping with the laws of war, minefields that were laid had to be documented on maps or aerial photos. After the helicopter had landed, the documents were passed to the unit command post that had given the order for the laying of the minefield. This unit then had to file the mine-laying record so that it could be used to remove the mines when the fighting had ended.

Border Patrols

For various reasons, guarding the nation's border enjoyed the highest priority in the German Democratic Republic. Mi-2 and Mi-8 helicopters of HS-16, the helicopter squadron of the border troops, patrolled the border areas from the air. In the 1980s, these patrols were as a rule carried out unarmed.

Since the Americans were flying patrols on the other side of the border, using armed AH-1 Cobra attack helicopters, in East Germany it was decided to respond with attack helicopters of their own. Helicopter-landing sites were built along the border, or existing sites were occupied by single Mi-8TBs or Mi-24s. These helicopters were kept in DHS (Diensthabendes System der Luftverteidigung) status, similar to NATO's QRA system.

Soviet and NVA helicopters waited on call to react to actions by the other side, but they also flew patrols along the border, during which, according to statements by those on the border, the Soviet pilots, like their American counterparts, did not always follow the border precisely.

There were occasionally mock duels along the border, one of which ended spectacularly in the crash of a Soviet Mi-24. The Western media used this incident as proof of the American AH-1 Cobra's superiority over the Soviet Mi-24. Soviet investigation reports confirm, however, that the Mi-24 pilot simply overstressed the helicopter during the engagement, pushing it beyond the allowable limits. In the process, the rotor blades bent so far that they struck the tail boom and were destroyed, making a crash unavoidable.

Border violations by civilian aircraft were a major annoyance for the East Germans. Although civilian air traffic was strongly regulated on the western side

It was not uncommon for Soviet Mi-24s to have to force Western private pilots to land after they flew into East German airspace. *Sergey Komarov via www.16va.be*

of the border between the two Germanys, some private pilots made a game of testing the Warsaw Pact's air defenses. They flew their Cessnas into East German airspace and waited for what must happen. The depths to which they penetrated were sometimes considerable. Flights were supposed to have been made as far as the Erfurt-Gera area and even into the Leipzig area.

As a rule, the Soviet air forces, which were chiefly responsible for the air defense of East Germany, dispatched jet interceptor fighters to force the Cessnas to land. When the MiGs appeared, the Cessnas reduced their airspeed to the point that they were flying slower than the MiGs' stall speeds allowed. Since the use of weapons was usually forbidden against an aircraft clearly identified as civilian, the MiGs had to break off their approach, gain speed, and make another pass. The West German private pilot used the time to turn away in the direction of home and escape. If necessary he repeated this procedure several times.

The rules of the game changed in the 1980s, and Mi-24s were increasingly used against penetrations into East German airspace by private aircraft. Since an Mi-24 was clearly faster and more maneuverable than any Cessna, the page turned and many hobby airspace violators were caught in the act and forced to land. There were of course often attempts to escape, but these usually ended the moment the civilian pilot found himself staring down the muzzles of a Yak-B machine gun pointed at his aircraft. In a very few cases, warning shots had to be fired to lend emphasis to the demand for an immediate landing. As a rule, the airspace violators were usually returned to the west side of the border after a relatively short time.

Intercept missions against slow-flying civilian intruders were carried out only by Soviet Mi-24s, and East German planes were not involved.

The Soviet Mi-24s were stationed on ten permanently or temporarily occupied landing fields along the western border. There were also the main airfields used by Soviet attack helicopter regiments, which were also not far from the border and from which patrols could also be flown if needed.

In the Berlin area there were two airfields, one north and one south of the city, that were used for patrols along the border with West Berlin.

NVA helicopters used their own airfields for DHS located near forward NVA radar sites or were temporarily based at helicopter landing fields used by the East German border patrol service. In addition to the Mi-24, the Mi-8TB also stood DHS. The DHS fields were always occupied by just a single helicopter. There were of course exceptions, such as the fields at Meinigen, Nordhausen, and Salzwedel, where HS-16's border units were permanently stationed.

Tactics in Afghanistan

Shortly before the turn of the year 1979–1980, the Soviet 40th Army overran Afghanistan. The Soviets quickly took control of the nation to keep their selected government in power. Senior American military men watched this operation with high regard and also a little envy, since those in the Pentagon believed they were seeing in the rapid Soviet advance a blueprint of how the United States could have decided the Vietnam War in its favor.

It soon turned out, however, that this thought construct was wrong. As the US in Vietnam had been literally stuck in a swamp, the Soviets soon found themselves confronted by seemingly impossible problems in the Afghan mountain land.

The Soviet Union assembled 110 helicopters for the conquest of Afghanistan, including ninety Mi-8 medium transport helicopters, a handful of Mi-6 heavy-lift helicopters, and a few Mi-2s that were used for reconnaissance and communications flights. The invasion was supported by just six Mi-24A strike helicopters. Nevertheless, the Soviets had all of Afghanistan in their hands within two weeks.

Resistance soon bestirred itself, however, and grew steadily stronger. The Mi-24s were used against partisans, and it was soon found that the Mi-24A,

with its inadequate armor protection, was ill suited to the task. In February 1980, therefore, an attack helicopter regiment with forty Mi-24Ds was sent to Afghanistan, The modern Mi-24 variants soon became the insurgents' nightmare, since there was little they could do against them with the small arms then available. The rebels, called *dushmani* by the Soviets, called the feared Mi-24 *sheitan arba*, which translates as "the devil's chariot." The statement by a *mujahideen* commander that the Afghans feared the Soviet soldiers less than their helicopters illustrates the Mi-24's effect on the enemy's morale.

The Mi-24D initially flew classic air strikes in support of Soviet ground forces. They operated singly, in pairs, or in small groups, and their main weapons at that stage of the war were unguided rockets, bombs, and the Yak-B machine gun. The minimum safe distance from friendly troops was 1,000 feet for the Yak-B machine gun, 1,640 feet for unguided rockets, and 4,920 feet for bombs.

If the need and opportunity arose, the Mi-24 could be used for free hunting. They were supposed to patrol a clearly defined area, search for enemy forces there, and, if possible, destroy them. The

dushmani quickly recognized that these Mi-24s had several problems at high altitudes, and moved their operations to those areas.

At high altitude the Mi-24D's performance was severely limited. It was unable to maneuver as well, and it was not possible for it to fly over high mountain peaks. Also, the bulk of the Mi-24 pilots sent to Afghanistan had no experience in flying in high mountains. A large percentage of the twenty-one Mi-24s lost in 1980 were the result of crashes that could be traced back to inadequate pilot training and insufficient engine power. After the introduction of improved engines, more-modern Mi-24 variants, and mountain flight training for pilots, the following year losses fell to just five. This time it was the 12.7 mm DShK machine gun, or *dushka* in soldier's jargon, that was responsible for the majority of losses. To escape the antiaircraft machine gun fire, the Mi-24s began carrying out long-range flights at altitudes outside the range of the *dushmani* air defense. Not until they had reached the area of operations did the helicopters descend to low altitude again.

While in the initial phase of the war in Afghanistan air support and free-hunting missions made up the bulk of the Mi-24's activities, from mid-1980 onward, escort flights began determining the day's events. The *dushmani* had begun to pull back from their direct confrontations with Soviet forces and turned instead to a classic guerrilla war, attacking the Soviet units' lines of communication. Mined roads, improvised explosive devices (IEDs), lone snipers, and massed ambushes subsequently became the order of the day in Afghanistan. The supply roads were soon littered with burned-out wrecks of vehicles.

The Mi-24 crews were given the job of protecting the supply convoys. They patrolled along the roads, searching for and engaging enemy forces. Since the convoys moved through the countryside at an average speed of just 9 to 12 mph, the escort flights were a time-consuming business that often went beyond the maximum flight endurance of the Mi-24. The Soviets were therefore forced to introduce mobile supply points. Temporary landing fields were set up along the roads, which were used to refuel and rearm the Mi-24s. Fuel and ammunition were either brought in by helicopter or by vehicles in the convoy.

As important as the escort flights were for the maintenance of the supply lines, they did tie down a considerable number of the attack helicopter units in Afghanistan.

More effective were escort flights dedicated to protecting airborne landings. Like the Americans in Vietnam, the Soviet forces also used the helicopter to quickly move troop contingents deep into enemy territory. More than sixty helicopters often took part in such large-scale airborne landing operations.

During these missions, the Mi-24s always had the task of being first to fly into enemy territory and taking out the air defenses there. Guided antitank missiles proved very effective since they could be fired from outside the range of enemy antiaircraft guns and struck their targets with great precision. Guided antitank missiles were also employed against fortified positions and bunkers. In the initial phase of the war, missiles with the usual hollow-charge warheads were used, but later missiles with fuel-air (thermobaric) warheads were used against these targets.

After firing their guided antitank missiles, the Mi-24s then began hitting the planned landing site with unguided rockets. Precision was less important; the area fire was intended only to keep the enemy's head down so that they could subsequently be engaged with bombs. Standard free-fall bombs were used at first, but starting in August 1980, the Soviet Mi-24s also began employing fuel-air bombs. While not always reliable, when they did work as they should, the effect

View from the front cockpit of an Mi-24 as the helicopter approaches an Afghan village. *Scheffler Collection*

was devastating. It was not for nothing that the local soldiers called them "the little man's atomic bomb."

Cluster bombs and other area weapons systems were also regularly used to engage enemy forces while clearing landing zones.

After the local resistance had been broken, the transport helicopters could fly into the combat zone and drop off the airborne troops. As this was happening, the Mi-24s circled, on the hunt for hostile forces.

When it was time to leave the landing zone, the Mi-24s remained on-site until the last transport helicopters had departed the area. In the air they then adopted a formation in which the Mi-24s led the way and, if necessary, opened the way with their forward-firing weapons. Cover to the sides and rear of the helicopter formation was the responsibility of the gunners on the Mi-8 / Mi-17 transport helicopters.

The first portable surface-to-air missiles appeared in the hands of the *dushmani* in 1982. They were Strela-2 missiles from stocks captured by the Israelis in Lebanon in 1982. These weapons made their way into the hands of the rebels by way of the US. The *mujahideen* were unable to achieve much with these weapons, since they lacked the training required for their successful use, but they did achieve several notable successes. These alarmed the Soviets, who immediately began equipping their helicopters with countermeasures.

Initially, all Mi-24s in the Afghan theater were fitted with two flare dispensers. These were mounted under the tail boom by using tension bands. Later, the number of dispensers was increased to four. The years 1983–84 saw the arrival of the AVU system, which blocked a direct view of the hot engine exhausts and swirled the exhaust gases in the rotor stream. This system was effective against the Strela and also the Redeye.

Mi-24s rose sharply in 1984. One reason for this was the Reagan administration's decision to provide the *mujahideen* with the FIM-92 Stinger, the latest portable surface-to-air missile. The arrival of the Stinger marked the beginning of a difficult period for the crews of the Mi-24s.

Gunsight view of an Afghan village. *Scheffler Collection*

The Stinger was so effective that the Soviet helicopter fleet in Afghanistan was temporarily paralyzed; however, Soviet special forces, the legendary *Spetsnaz*, quickly succeeded in capturing examples of the Stinger. They were sent to the Soviet Union, where they were quickly analyzed. The researchers discovered weaknesses in the Stinger and on the basis of these were able to develop effective countermeasures.

With the appearance of the Stinger, the Mi-24 crews were given a new, important, but unpopular assignment. Since the *dushmani* shot at everything that flew, including transport and passenger aircraft approaching an Afghan airfield the Mi-24s had to ensure that passenger and transport aircraft could land safely.

Pairs of Mi-24s were assigned to keep watch on areas surrounding airfields, looking out for suspicious activity. The most unpleasant task went to the pair of Mi-24s that had to rendezvous with the civil aircraft at higher altitude. The Mi-24s took up position on both sides of the civil aircraft and began a steep descent to land, protecting it with their bodies. Flares were released continuously during the approach to provide permanent protection against infrared-guided missiles. If a portable surface-to-air missile was launched, the Mi-24 pilots had orders to do whatever was required to prevent it from reaching its target. In case of doubt, the Mi-24 pilots were to place their helicopters between incoming missiles and passenger aircraft and take the hit themselves. This in fact happened a number of times during the war in Afghanistan.

In the vast majority of cases, the helicopter crews were able to protect passenger or transport aircraft— but not always.

The most critical phase of the war in Afghanistan for the helicopter units was the first half of 1987. Stingers were arriving in the country in large numbers, and in the first six months of 1987, the Soviet attack helicopter units lost more Mi-24s than they had in all of the previous year. Modern countermeasures became available. The infrared jammers, which had recently entered service, could be tuned to jam the Stinger's seeker head almost perfectly. The effectiveness of flares and the AVU system had also been improved. In conjunction with other countermeasures, from then on the effectiveness of the FIM-92 Stinger was sharply reduced. Just three more Mi-24s were written off as total losses in the second half of 1987. In 1988 and 1989, Soviet Mi-24 losses were reduced to three per year. The thorn of the Stinger had been pulled.

Stinger surface-to-air missiles captured by *Spetsnaz* troops. *Scheffler Collection*

The strict use of a new tactic, in which Mi-24 attack helicopters and specialized Mi-17s worked together, also played a major role in reducing losses. While the Mi-24s covered the front of a helicopter formation, the Mi-17s guarded the formation's flanks and rear.

The highly regarded Russian periodical *Mir Aviatsiya* put the number of Mi-24s irretrievably lost during the war in Afghanistan at 122, with the highest annual losses taking place in 1980 and 1987, with twenty-one helicopters written off in each of those years.

The majority of Mi-24s shot down fell prey to heavy machine guns. In total, 42 percent of all of the downed helicopters went to the *dushkas*, and another 25 percent were destroyed by light antiaircraft guns. Of the remaining 33 percent, 3 percent were shot down by small-arms fire, and 30 percent were brought down by portable surface-to-air missiles.

The loss rate could have been higher had it not been for the Mi-24's robust and hit-absorbing design, as well as the self-sacrificial work of the ground personnel, who worked around the clock to keep the attack helicopters operational in Afghanistan.

The harsh conditions in Afghanistan made high demands of men and machines. Constant dust and blowing sand caused the technology to wear more rapidly; the rate of wear was very high. There was also Afghanistan's extreme continental climate. It was very hot in summer, but bitterly cold in winter. Many regions also contain high mountains, which hampered operations by attack helicopters.

On hot summer days, the Mi-24 had difficulties taking off from airfields at high elevations. The thin air combined with the high temperatures made a conventional vertical takeoff almost impossible. Since the troops still required air support, the helicopters made rolling takeoffs. This procedure was very effective, drastically improving the helicopters' maximum payload. It appeared in none of the service or flight manuals, however. Since the military required everything to be in order, the OKB Mil was tasked with certifying the rolling-takeoff procedure.

To simulate conditions at high elevations in Afghanistan, an Mi-24 selected for trials was overloaded. It ultimately weighed 2.2 tons more than the allowable maximum takeoff weight. In a television report, the test pilot recalled that he applied power, allowed the helicopter to begin rolling, then pushed the stick forward. "It was a strange feeling when the rear of the helicopter rose and all the weight rested on the nosewheel, while the helicopter was moving forward. The main rotor sank, and just as I thought it was about to touch the ground, the Mi-24 rose gently into the air." This happened about 120 to 150 feet after the start of the takeoff run.

The results of these tests were surprising. As crazy as the takeoff procedure sounded, it worked perfectly. There were also no problems with the technology.

Although the nosewhcel had not been designed for the high loads it had to bear during this takeoff procedure, it handled them with ease. The takeoff procedure was approved and from then on was used officially in Afghanistan.

БОЕВЫЕ ПОТЕРИ ПО ТИПАМ К 15.02.89 г.								
Год	Самолеты					Вертолеты		
	МиГ-21, МиГ-23	Су-17	Су-25, Су-24	Ан-12, Ан-26, Ан-30, Ил-76	Всего	Ми-6, Ми-10	Ми-8	Ми-24	Всего
1980	3	1	-	1+1**	4	2	19	21	42
1981	1	2	1	-	4	-	17	5	22
1982	6	1	-	-	7	4	20	9	33
1983	2	3	1	1	7	2	16	7	25
1984	1	7	2	1	10	6	21	18	45
1985	4	3	1	3	11	6	26	21	53
1986	1	7	8	2	18	5	25	17	47
1987	2	4	8	3	17	3	24	21	48
1988	-	2	1+1*	1	2	-	2	3	5
1989	-	-	1	1	2	-	2	3	5
Всего	20	30	22	9	80	28	170	122	320

Один Су-24 (*) и один Ил-76 (**), потерю которых, по всем признакам, можно отнести к боевым, не учтены в официальной сводке боевых потерь.
Разница между официальными данными и данными, приведёнными в таблице (107-80=27 самолетов и 333-320=13 вертолетов), есть потери, отнесённые к небоевым. Это следствие пожаров на стоянках, аварийных посадок, ошибок при наземном обслуживании, конструктивных и производственных дефектов и пр.

List of total Mi-24 losses in Afghanistan to February 15, 1989, compiled by Mir Aviatsiy. Column 8 shows Mi-24 losses.
US DoD

The Mi-24 and the Attack Helicopters of the West

From its conception, the Mi-24 was a unique design. It had no direct counterpart among the helicopters of the Western nations. The Bell AH-1 Cobra has a comparable service life, and also comparable was the Lockheed AH-56 Cheyenne, because the Mi-24 was designed in response to that helicopter. Also comparable is the Sikorsky S-67 Blackhawk, whose layout is most similar.

AH-1: Simple, Underrated, and Yet Amazingly Capable

The Mi-24 is often seen as the direct counterpart of the AH-1 Cobra. This may be true with respect to time frame, since the two helicopter types have formed the backbones of their countries' attack helicopter units for a long time and therefore faced each other in the heart of Europe.

The Cobra was an interim solution; Bell had been working on studies for a true attack helicopter since the end of the 1950s. In 1963, it created the Bell 207 Sioux Scout, a helicopter that during the course of a feasibility study convinced the US military of the value of an attack helicopter. But when the US Department of Defense organized a competition for a future American attack helicopter in 1964, Bell's Model 209 lost out to the Lockheed CL-840 Cheyenne. Bell refused to admit defeat, however, and in early 1965, it invested in further development of the Model 209.

By that time the war in Vietnam had intensified, and the absence of a capable attack helicopter was making itself felt. Since Lockheed's Cheyenne could not become available in the foreseeable future, the US Army requested submissions from five companies for a simple attack helicopter that could be made available quickly.

CHAPTER 7

Bell immediately began working on a prototype, which made its first flight on September 7, 1965. A month later it set a speed record for helicopters. In April 1966, the Model 209 emerged victorious from comparison flights against the other competitors, whereupon the US Army placed an order for 110 aircraft. From then on, the official type designation was AH-1, and its official name, contrary to the tradition of naming army helicopters after American Indian tribes, was Huey Cobra. This was thought of as a reference to the armed UH-1s operating in Vietnam, which were called Cobras, but also as an indication that the AH-1 was seen only as an interim measure to bridge the gap until the AH-56 became available. But as we know, temporary arrangements often have long lives.

The AH-1 did well in Vietnam. It did outstanding work and was an important support for the fighting troops, this despite the fact that it lacked advanced weapons and sensors. The Cobra was a simple, reliable, and powerful strike helicopter tailored to the conditions of the jungle war.

With the Vietnam War lost, and the Cheyenne still not available, for better or worse the Cobra had to enter service in Europe. However, it was not really suited for its assigned role there. The AH-1G, the Vietnam variant, was incapable of halting armored attacks, and consequently the TOW (tube-launched, optically tracked, wire-guided) antitank missile system was quickly developed and a more advanced version of the Cobra, the AH-1Q, was placed in service.

When development of the Cheyenne was canceled, the Cobra was forced to fill in until the arrival of the AH-64 Apache. It underwent a series of upgrades and through the AH-1S, P, and E versions was brought up to AH-1F standard. It remained in service with the US Army until 1999. Twin-engined Cobra variants remain in service with the US Navy and the US Marine Corps to the present day.

This was an impressive career for a helicopter that the military initially did not even want.

Compared to the Mi-24, the Cobra is smaller, lighter, and slower. The Cobra also does not climb as fast and cannot carry as heavy a weapons load as the Mi-24.

The most modern version of the Cobra is the AH-1Z used by the Marine Corps. *US Navy, Adler*

The Cobra and the Mi-24 faced each other in combat just once, during the Iran-Iraq War, which at the time was called the Gulf War, before this name was given to another military conflict. If the reports can be believed, and there is reason for skepticism, there were various clashes in which guided antitank missiles were used to engage opposing helicopters. The Iraqi Mi-24s are supposed to have shot down ten Cobras, while just six Mi-24s fell victim to the Cobras. The Iraqis also claim that an Mi-24 succeeded in shooting down an F-4E Phantom. As has been said, there is definitely reason for skepticism.

AH-56A Cheyenne, Lockheed's High-Tech Helicopter

Lockheed won the AAFSS (Advanced Aerial Fire Support System) competition for the US Army's future attack helicopter with its project CL-840. A very advanced design technologically, it combined elements of the helicopter and gyrocopter. Takeoff, landing, and low-speed flight were accomplished with the rotor, like a normal helicopter, but for high-speed flight the main rotor was uncoupled and propulsion, like a gyrocopter, was provided by a pusher propeller at the end of the aircraft's tail boom. During high-speed flight, the stub wings generated much of the lift. This enabled the Cheyenne to fly at very high speeds. In level flight it could achieve between 242 and 252 mph, while in a fast dive it was capable of reaching top speeds between 280 and 300 mph.

The AH-56A was equipped with a 7.62 mm rotary machine gun in a revolving nose turret and a 30 mm cannon in a rotating belly turret. It was capable of carrying unguided rockets and TOW antitank missiles.

The Cheyenne had a highly advanced sensor system and onboard computer. The pilot could aim the cannon by using a helmet sight, while the gunner, in a rotating seat, always faced in the direction in which the machine guns were pointing.

The AH-56A program had to battle many technical problems, resulting in delays and budget overruns. When one prototype crashed and another missed most of its targets during a demonstration for senior military men, the project was canceled.

When the Mi-24 was developed, the AH-56 Cheyenne was the yardstick against which it was measured. The Mi-24 was a little larger and heavier than the Cheyenne. It was also not as fast and did not climb as well. The payloads of the two helicopters were comparable, with the Cheyenne being able to carry a greater number of guided antitank missiles. The Cheyenne was also clearly superior when it came to sensor systems. In terms of reliability and robustness, however, it could not keep up with the Mi-24.

The AH-56A was seen as a benchmark in the development of the Mi-24.
Lockheed

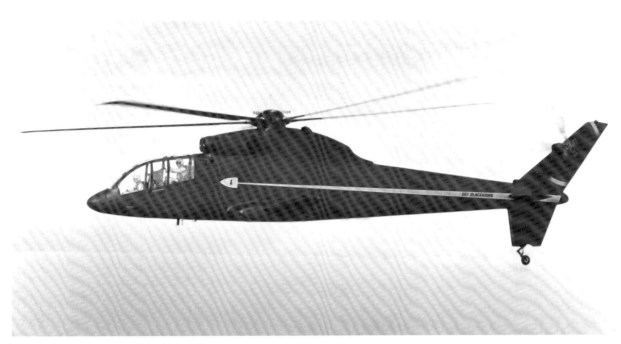

The elegant Sikorsky S-67 Blackhawk was the Western attack helicopter whose shape was most reminiscent of the Mi-24. *Sikorsky*

Sikorsky's Gem, the S-67 Blackhawk

Sikorsky took part in the AAFSS competition with its S-66 project, which proved inferior to the AH-56. When the AH-56 program began encountering more-frequent problems, Sikorsky decided to continue development at its own risk and gave it the project designation S-67 Blackhawk.

The goal was to develop a fast-flying attack helicopter that met the army's requirements. To minimize development risks, the S-67 used proven components from the S-61. The five-blade rotor, for example, was a variant of the S-61's main rotor, while the tail rotor was taken directly from the earlier helicopter. The S-67's airframe was streamlined to allow it to reach high speeds, and the undercarriage was retractable.

Unusual for a helicopter was the design of the stub wings; they were equipped with speed brakes and control surfaces, which led to a clear improvement in maneuverability.

The S-67 was armed with an automatic cannon in a rotating turret. The main armament could be carried on four underwing stores stations. Each station was prepared to accommodate a quadruple launcher for TOW weapons. They could also carry unguided rockets, bombs, and cannon pods.

The S-67's development progressed quickly, and design work began in November 1969. Work on the prototype began in February 1970, and its first flight took place on August 20, 1970.

Just one prototype was built, and it carried out all flight testing, including comparison flights against the AH-56A Cheyenne and the Bell 309 KingCobra.

The S-67 was a large helicopter, but despite this it was maneuverable and easy to fly, and pilots praised its handling.

In 1970, the S-67 set two world speed records. Despite its outstanding performance the US Army rejected the S-67.

The Mi-24 and S-67 resembled one another in configuration. Both had their power plants forward of the main rotor and a large glazed cockpit. The S-67 was larger and heavier than the Mi-24A but had less powerful engines. It did, however, have a more favorable aerodynamic shape, and the maximum speeds and rates of climb for both helicopters were almost identical. The Mi-24 had superior range, but the S-67 was capable of carrying a greater weapons load.

Also, the S-67's elegant lines were captivating.

Some publications have stated that the S-67 had a cargo compartment capable of accommodating up to four soldiers. In this respect it was a conceptual counterpart to the Mi-24.

AH-64A Apache

In 1972, the AAFSS competition was canceled because the leaders of the US Army believed that the conditions under which a war in central Europe would be fought had changed significantly. The armored units of the Warsaw Pact, whose decimation was seen as the primary objective of the American attack helicopter, had acquired a modern defensive shield against air attack through the creation of a modern air defense system. Large numbers of mobile surface-to-air missiles of various ranges, which moved with the armored units, combined with highly mobile ZSU-23-4 Shilka self-propelled antiaircraft weapons systems for short-range defense, made the previous operational tactics used by attack helicopters obsolete.

During development of the AH-56, S-67, and KingCobra attack helicopters, the US military had assumed that the helicopters would approach at medium to low altitude, launch their guided antitank missiles from a distance, then quickly and aggressively approach to firing range for their unguided rockets and cannon and overwhelm the enemy. In principle this thinking was not dissimilar to the operational principles of the Mi-24.

With the growing strength of the Soviet frontline air defenses, the US Army no longer considered this tactic a viable one. Instead, henceforth the attack helicopters would creep up on the enemy by using nap-of-the earth (NOE) tactics, rise briefly from cover, fire their weapons from a hover, and then disappear again as quickly as possible.

None of the AAFSS seemed really suitable for the new tactic, which is why a new competition titled AAH (Advanced Attack Helicopter) was begun. Hughes won the competition with its Model 77. The first YAH-64 prototype took to the air for the first time on September 30, 1975, and in 1984 the helicopter entered production as the AH-64A Apache.

The AH-64A Apache was a highly innovative helicopter design, the first in the history of American attack helicopters to have extensive armor protection. Advanced observation and sensor technology, paired with capable computer systems and a powerful armament, made the AH-64A Apache the most capable attack helicopter in the 1980s. It was a generation ahead of the Mi-24s then in use.

The AH-64A was smaller and lighter than the Mi-24. Its engines were slightly less powerful, and the Apache was also slower than the Mi-24. The climb

performance of both helicopters was about the same. Weapons payload was almost identical, but the AH-64A could carry more guided weapons. The AH-64A's armor protection was also superior.

The AH-64A could justifiably be regarded as the American answer to the Mi-24. Interestingly, experience

A Czech Mi 24V and an American AH-64D in formation. *US Army, Chlebecek*

in Iraq showed that the US Army's preferred tactic of attacking from a hover resulted in heavier losses than the previous assault tactic, which was still practiced by the attack helicopters of the US Marine Corps. In Afghanistan the AH-64 pilots returned to the assault tactic because it was found that moving helicopters were not hit as frequently as those that remained in a hover. The AH-64 thus quasi-adapted the tactics that the Soviet Mi-24s had used in the same terrain years before.

The Mi-24 Worldwide

Worldwide Distribution

I f one uses the number of user states as a yardstick, the Mi-24 is the most widely used attack helicopter in the world today. It is operated by the militaries of countries on five continents, flying in Europe, Asia, Africa, North America, and South America.

The Mi-24 was initially designed for use exclusively by the Soviet military. The Mi-24A therefore wore only the red star of the Soviet air forces. As regards red stars, in the West it was generally believed that the red star adorned every vehicle, every tank, every ship, and every aircraft of the Soviet Army. This is true in part, if one looks at Soviet ships, helicopters, and fixed-wing aircraft. Vehicles, however, whether trucks, four-wheel-drive vehicles, or tanks, as a rule did not wear individual red stars as nationality emblems; rather, they were a subordinate part of a larger emblem. National insignia were often not present on vehicles; instead there were cryptic letter-number combinations that indicated, for instance, the vehicle's unit. But back to the Mi-24.

When the Mi-24D first became available, the Soviet army had begun phasing out the Mi-24A. Numerous examples were passed on to Vietnam, Algeria, Afghanistan, and Ethiopia. The Mi-24A received its baptism of fire in Ethiopian service. That was the Ogaden War in 1977, which was fought against the neighboring state of Somalia.

The Mi-24D began spreading widely in 1978. It was approved for export and delivered to the states of the Warsaw Pact. In the years that followed, the Mi-24D entered service in large numbers with East Germany, Poland, Czechoslovakia, Hungary, and Bulgaria. Only Romania did not procure the Mi-24, preferring to develop its own attack helicopter and failing miserably thanks to its own hubris. The Mi-24 remained the backbone of the attack helicopter forces of the other Warsaw Pact states until the fall of the Soviet Union near the end of 1991. In the late 1980s, the Warsaw Pact countries began receiving the more modern Mi-24 variants such as the Mi-24V and P.

Active and former user states of the Mi-24.

CHAPTER 8

The Mi-24 continued in operation long after the political upheavals. Bulgaria and Hungary recently mothballed their machines for cost reasons, as did Slovakia, which after Czechoslovakia split into the Czech Republic and the Slovak Republic received its Mi-24s from Czechoslovakian stocks. The Czech Republic continues to use the Mi-24 to the present day. The same is true of Germany's neighbor to the east, Poland, where the Mi-24 continues to serve faithfully.

Cyprus procured new Mi-35Ps and uses them within its national guard.

In the Yugoslavian successor states, Croatia received several Mi-24Vs in convoluted ways and used them successfully against Serbian rebels. These aircraft have been mothballed since 2002. Macedonia took a similar path, but there it was Albanian or Kosovar rebels against which the Mi-24Vs were used.

In the successor states to the Soviet Union, the Mi-24 still serves in large numbers. Whether in Russia, White Russia, the Ukraine, Kazakhstan, Turkmenistan, Kirgizia, Uzbekistan, Armenia, Georgia, or Azerbaijan, numerically the Mi-24 is still the best-represented attack helicopter. In many states of the former Soviet Union, modernization measures are underway to extend the lives of the machines and upgrade their capabilities. Some successor states have purchased new-build, modern Mi-35Ms.

In East Ukraine and the Caucasus, the Mi-24 saw action in military confrontations; in some cases Mi-24 met Mi-24. In the central Asian republics, the Mi-24 was used to combat Islamic rebels.

Only the three Baltic States have no Mi-24s in their inventories. They essentially have no air forces of their own, which is why NATO assumed responsibility for air defense over the Baltic States.

Mi-24Ds were downgraded to Mi-25 standard for export to the Third World. They were initially sold in the Middle East; Syria, Libya, and Iraq all operate the type. The Mi-25s were involved in wars in all three states. In 1982 Syrian Mi-25s successfully fought against Israel, Iraqi machines were used against Iran between 1980 and 1988, and Libya's unconventional dictator Gaddafi sent his Mi-25s to Chad. The Mi-25 also went to Algeria and was delivered to South Yemen.

In Asia, North Korea received the Mi-25. As a loyal ally of the Soviet Union, Vietnam received the Mi-24D. Mongolia, which had to be seen as a political appendage of the USSR, also obtained Mi-24Ds. India first procured the Mi-25 and later the Mi-35 as well. These aircraft were modernized with Israeli help. The Afghan military received various versions of the Mi-24 from Soviet stocks and today, with the support of American advisors, operate the Mi-35.

After the fall of the Soviet Union, Sri Lanka and Indonesia obtained Mi-24s from surplus stocks. At the beginning of the twenty-first century, Myanmar ordered new Mi-35M helicopters.

In southern Africa, Angola and Mozambique are considered progressive states. Their armed forces were equipped with Mi-25s, some of which were flown by Cuban pilots in Angola.

After the collapse of the Soviet Union, states of the Commonwealth of Independent States (a.k.a. the Russian Commonwealth) began selling off surplus Mi-24s, and many African states used the opportunity to procure a capable attack helicopter relatively cheaply. Today, therefore, the Mi-24 is widely spread in Africa. Operator states include Chad, the Sudan, Zimbabwe, Sierra Leone, Rwanda, Uganda, and Nigeria, to name but a few. Ukrainian Mi-24Ps also fly in Africa as part of UN peacekeeping missions.

On the American continent, Cuba was the first to receive the Mi-24D. In the mid-1980s, these aircraft went to Nicaragua's Sandinista regime, which used them in its struggle against the US-financed and US-equipped Contra rebels.

Peru, a longtime customer for Soviet war materiel, also procured the Mi-25. These aircraft were overhauled and modernized in Russia in 2011. Peru also obtained updated Mi-35P helicopters. New customers in South America were Venezuela, the first customer for the Mi-35, and Brazil, which began receiving Mi-35s in 2009.

Interestingly, the US military also operates the Mi-24, but only to represent hostile aircraft. They procured a number of Mi-24s from eastern European NATO countries and the Federal Republic of Germany. In 1991, Germany gave one Mi-24D and one Mi-24P to the US.

American Mi-24s

In the 1970s and 1980s, the NATO military forces had tremendous respect for the mighty Mi-24, and for good reason. The Mi-24 could do things that no Eastern helicopter could. It was amazingly agile, amazingly powerful, and also could even transport troops.

In the late 1970s, in the American West near the gaming paradise of Las Vegas, a huge training area was created from the ground up, on which to practice for the Third World War. American combat pilots met real MiGs and F-5E Tigers, which simulated Soviet tactics. On the ground there were American units equipped with Soviet technology or American vehicles adapted to simulate Soviet technology that used Soviet tactics to simulate the enemy. They met regular American units and showed them how the enemy fought, often very successfully.

The air force maneuvers were called Red Flag, and those of the US Army were called OPFOR, which stood for OPposing FORces.

To make the OPFOR maneuvers as realistic as possible, it was necessary to simulate the Mi-24. Real Mi-24s were not as easy to come by as MiG-21s, which the Americans had simply purchased from the Indonesians and Egyptians. They were therefore forced to convert their own helicopters to resemble the Mi-24. Several UH-1s were equipped with special radar reflectors to simulate the radar signature of the Mi-24.

These UH-1s bore no similarity to the Mi-24, however. Several S-55s were therefore modified to visually simulate the Mi-24. They were fitted with a fiberglass nose with the characteristic shape of the Mi-24, including dual cockpits and a dummy crew. Stub wings were installed, along with mockups of the armament.

While these fake Hinds resembled the Mi-24 externally, their performance was nothing like that of the real Mi-24.

In 1985, the Americans finally got their hands on an Mi-24D, or, to be more accurate, Mi-25s from Libyan stocks, which had been captured by the French in Chad.

The Mi-24D was examined and tested by an excellent helicopter pilot. After some initial difficulties the pilot was able to quickly get used to the Mi-24, and at the conclusion of testing he stated that the Mi-24 was the best helicopter he had ever flown.

Converted S-55 helicopters designated QS-55 simulated the Mi-24 during OPFOR training missions. *US DoD*

Mi-24V in American service. Note the triple-barrel machine gun. *US DoD*

After the political upheavals in eastern Europe, the US procured numerous Mi-24s and to this day uses them to represent the enemy. American expertise on the subject of the Mi-24 has reached such a level that the US military regularly trains other states (e.g., Afghanistan and Iraq) to operate the Mi-24.

The army used converted UH-1s to represent Mi-24s. *US DoD*

Mi-24P of the
American OPFOR
units. *USAF,
S. Turner*

The Mi-24 in German Service

At the beginning of the 1970s, the Soviet Union demanded that its allies make greater efforts to strengthen the offensive capabilities of their air forces.

This resulted in the formation of the first fighter-bomber wing in East Germany. This was a first step, but it was far from enough for the big brother from Moscow. The Soviets constantly and vehemently kept up their demands for increased offensive capabilities and modernization in the air until the end of the German Democratic Republic (GDR). But it was also in the NVA's own interests to have capable aviation units that could provide the land forces with direct air support. The formation of an attack helicopter wing was an obvious choice.

The germ cell of the new unit was the 5th Squadron of Helicopter Wing 34 (HG-34) at Brandenburg-Briest. The squadron was equipped with armed Mi-2 and Mi-8T helicopters, and these were to be used to retrain pilots and gunners for their new roles.

The unit was officially activated on November 1, 1975, and received the designation Helicopter Wing 54, or HG-54 for short. On November 21, 1975, HG-54 moved to its own newly created helicopter base at Basepohl near Brandenburg, which was to be the wing's home from that time onward.

In the late summer of 1976, helicopters of the new unit took part in large-scale maneuvers for the first time. That was its first real trial by fire, but with armed Mi-2s and Mi-8Ts it was not really capable of providing effective air support. But help was on the way. The first heavily armed and armored Mi-8TBs arrived in February 1977, and in August 1978 the unit received its first four Mi-24Ds. As the USSR's most trusted ally, East Germany was the first country outside the Soviet Union to receive the new attack helicopter. This was noted with approval by the leaders of the GDR.

In 1979, the wing received four more Mi-24Ds. On October 7, 1979, seven Mi-24s took part in the parade in honor of the thirtieth anniversary of the GDR in Berlin. The western allies subsequently complained loudly to the Soviets, and an aerial parade was never again carried out.

On March 1, 1980, NVA Day, HG-54 was given the traditional name Adolf von Lützow. The choice of name

Mi-24D of the NVA. Aircraft 520 was delivered in August 1981, and logged 1,815 hours in service with the National People's Army. After it was received by the *Bundeswehr* it was given the code 96+09. *Rob Schleiffert*

demonstrated a new trend in the NVA: new units were no longer named for communist heroes, but rather for heroes of the war of liberation against Napoleon.

By April 30, 1981, pilot training had reached such an advanced stage that the helicopter wing was taken into the Warsaw Pact's on-duty system. It had officially reached full combat status. During 1981, the wing received an additional eighteen Mi-24Ds. The relationship between the Mi-8TB and the Mi-24D shifted decisively in favor of the attack helicopter, and this development was also reflected in the unit designation. On December 1, 1981, Attack Helicopter Wing 57, or KHG-57, was created from HG-54.

At about the same time, a second attack helicopter wing was created. At Brandenburg-Briest, Attack Helicopter Wing 67 (KHG-67) was formed from Helicopter Squadron 64 (HS-64); this unit was initially equipped with Mi-8TBs. KHG-67 received the Mi-24D on June 19, 1982. Since Brandenburg-Briest was under the western air corridor to West Berlin and the Americas, the British and French exploited the situation for air intelligence gathering, and in November 1982, KHG-67 moved to Cottbus. The airfield there had been left by Fighter Wing 1 because the city had grown so much in the 1970s that the approaches to the runways passed over residential areas. A fatal accident, in which an MiG-21 crashed into an apartment building, made the untenability of the situation obvious to all. *JG 1* subsequently moved to the newly established airfield at Holzdorf, and KHG-67 took over the field at Cottbus. It remained the attack helicopter wing's base until the end of the GDR.

On October 7, 1984, the wing was awarded the title *Ferdinand von Schiller*.

Both attack helicopter wings were equipped with one squadron of Mi-8TBs and one of Mi-24Ds. Each also had a third squadron that was responsible for special duties such as command and reconnaissance. Both squadrons also had their own maintenance and repair sections, which were responsible for minor periodic checks and repairs. Major checks and repairs were carried out by the VEB aircraft maintenance facility in Dresden.

By 1983, the Soviets had delivered a total of 42 Mi-24Ds to East Germany, which served both with KHG-57 at Basepohl and KHG-67 at Cottbus.

The Mi-24D was an enormous step forward for the NVA. The ability of the NVA air force (LaSK) to support its own land forces (LSK) in battle rose considerably.

It soon turned out, however, that cooperation between the LSK and the LaSK was not without its difficulties. In 1982, therefore, the FO FAFK command organization was created, in which officers of the land forces were supposed to work with the wings of the LSK. KHG-57 was attached to this command organization on September 30, 1982.

By the end of 1984, the development had reached the point that both attack helicopter wings were removed from the organization of the LSK and made part of the land forces, which took place on November 30, 1984. The army air force had become a reality.

To document the new command relationship, on December 1, 1986, the wings were given new designations: KHG-57 became KHG-5 and KHG-67 was renamed KHG-3. The new numbers corresponded to the numbers of the military districts in East Germany, which in case of war would have formed the 3rd and 5th Armies of the Warsaw Pact. Basing of the units at Basepohl and Cottbus remained unchanged.

Although the attack helicopter wings were officially and structurally part of the army, their members still wore the uniform of the air force. Its personnel continued to be trained at the LSK schools, and technical support was provided by the air force.

The introduction of the Mi-24D took place quickly and was largely unproblematic. The new helicopter was displayed publicly for the first time in 1979, during a military display for the leaders of the party and state. By September 1980, enough Mi-24s had been delivered and crews trained for HG-54 to take part in the major military exercise dubbed Brothers in Arms 80, which was held in East Germany.

During the maneuvers, the crews demonstrated that they could repulse and destroy armored advances by the enemy with their Mi-24Ds. The NVA had achieved operational readiness with a completely new weapons system in an amazingly short time.

But not everything went smoothly. The first fatal accident involving the Mi-24D occurred on August 26, 1980, when during a training flight the crew got carried away by the Mi-24D's excellent flight characteristics and overstressed the airframe. The accident was originally blamed on a bird strike, but closer examination revealed that during the aggressive execution of a maneuver, the rotor blades had bent so far that they struck the tail boom and were destroyed. A crash was unavoidable and the crew was killed. It

was the first and only time that an Mi-24D of the NVA experienced this misfortune. The Soviet forces had often encountered this problem, but the information never made its way to the pilots of the NVA's attack helicopters. Additional manuals and handling instructions were therefore purchased from the Soviet Union, and the documents were fully translated from Russian into German. Flight parameter limitations were contained in these documents. A bit of wisdom shared by Soviet pilots that still circulates among Russian Mi-24 pilots today proved true: "If you know exactly what you want to do with an Mi-24 and especially what you should avoid at all costs, then the Crocodile is the best attack helicopter in the world!"

Another fatal accident took place on June 3, 1982, when the Mi-24D with the tactical number "521" carried out a hover near the bank of the Havel River. The unfortunate combination of high temperature and unexpected air currents resulted in the main rotor striking trees standing on the bank. The rotor was destroyed, leading to a crash. The pilot was killed, but the gunner and the flight engineer survived and after recovering returned to duty.

Aircraft 396 was delivered in May 1981. In *Bundeswehr* service it wore the code 96+02. *Rob Schleiffert*

487 with servicing hatches open. The helicopter was delivered in July 1981. In *Bundeswehr* service it wore the code 96+07. *Rob Schleiffert*

Mi-24D "521" was recovered and repaired, but it was never returned to flying status. Instead it was sent to the Harry Kuhn Military School in Bad Düben, where it was used as a training aid for prospective helicopter technicians.

At Bad Düben the aircraft was given the new tactical number "5211," and this became the only NVA helicopter with a four-digit bort number. Today "5211" can be seen in the Gatow air museum.

A takeoff accident on August 24, 1984, had relatively minor consequences. The starboard engine failed during takeoff, and the helicopter descended and came down hard. Parts of the undercarriage collapsed, but the damage was repairable and the crew escaped with a fright.

The last loss of an Mi-24D, which occurred on October 26, 1984, was more tragic, however. An Mi-24D was at a forward airfield near the border with the Federal Republic of Germany on a routine deployment. On the day it was relieved, there was dense fog with visibility below 150 feet. Since there was adequate visibility at the helicopter's home base at Cottbus, the crew made an instrument takeoff to

fly back to its base. In the process the Mi-24 collided with a cable bracing the radio mast of a Soviet fighter control station (other sources say a radar site). The collision unfortunately resulted in the entire cockpit section being severed when the helicopter crashed and burned. The flight engineer had the good fortune to be thrown clear when the helicopter broke up, and he survived with serious injuries.

As previously mentioned, deliveries of the Mi-24D continued until 1983. There were whispers that before being delivered to East Germany, some of these helicopters had been sent directly from the factory to Afghanistan for intensive field testing. This testing was done without the knowledge of the Germans.

A variation of the story relates that the first four Mi-24s delivered were sent back to Moscow for a major periodic check and that the inspection took an unusually long time. After several inquiries to the manufacturer, where the Mi-24s supposedly were, the helicopters returned to Basepohl. The NVA authorities were initially not sure that Moscow had returned the right helicopters. There were repaired bullet holes and other damage that had not been there before. The fresh paint appeared to have been sprayed right over a layer of dust, since it was possible to feel grains of sand under the paint.

After the serial numbers on the airframe and engines had been checked, it was found that they were in fact the NVA aircraft. When the manufacturer was asked what had happened to the NVA's Mi-24Ds, after several glasses of tongue-loosening vodka had been consumed, its representatives secretly spoke about factory trials in Afghanistan.

Many contemporary witnesses doubt this story, and it should be taken with a grain of salt. What is known, however, is that from then on, all major checks and repairs on Mi-24s of the NVA were carried out by the VEB aircraft maintenance facility in Dresden.

By the mid-1980s, the Falanga guided antitank missile system was rapidly becoming obsolete since the armored units of the NATO countries were fielding growing numbers of modern, well-protected tanks such as the Leopard 2 and M1 Abrams. Falanga-P was not capable of penetrating the frontal armor of these vehicles. Attempts to hit the vulnerable top armor were more a matter of luck than a realistic option. The GDR therefore began efforts to obtain more-modern versions of the Mi-24 for its attack helicopter wings.

Deliveries were slow in coming, however. The reason behind this was the personal animosity between the heads of the party and state in East Germany and the Soviet Union. Honecker and Gorbachov did not like one another. Gorbachov treated the regime of elderly gentlemen from Wandlitz with condescension, and Honecker, unlike most of the East German population, did not think much of Gorbachov's policy of glasnost and perestroika and also let him know it. Statements such as "He should first try to fill his country's shops, before he tells us how to build socialism," have been authenticated. Gorbachov reacted to this insubordination huffily. He caused East Germany to be refused delivery of certain modern weapons systems for flimsy excuses or delayed their delivery. The NVA received neither the T-80 battle tank nor the long-promised, large-scale delivery of BMP-2 armored personnel carriers. The modern Mi-24s were also held back, the reason given being that the Soviet Union needed them more urgently in Afghanistan and could therefore not deliver them.

This caused disgruntlement in the GDR because at the same time, the Soviet Union was delivering the BMP-2 armored personnel carrier and Mi-35 (export version of the Mi-24V) attack helicopters to Iraq and other states. The difference was that these countries paid in American dollars, while the GDR could offer only foreign-exchange rubles.

To appease the upset leadership of the GDR, in the 1980s Moscow decided to finally provide modern

Aircraft 522, delivered in August 1981, flew 1,763 hours in NVA service. With the *Bundeswehr* it wore the code 96+10. *Rob Schleiffert*

Servicing an NVA
Mi-24. *Air Force
Museum, Gatow*

Servicing an NVA Mi-24. *Air Force Museum, Gatow*

equipment to the East German air force. The modern MiG-29A fighter aircraft and the Mi-24P attack helicopter entered service with the NVA. As a broad indication, the GDR received the new military technology, but not as a "brother state." It was Moscow's way of demonstrating that East Germany was no longer regarded as the Soviet Union's closest ally.

At the end of 1985, KHG-5 at Basepohl received the first twelve Mi-24Ps. Deliveries of additional aircraft of this type were promised for 1990, as well as the delivery of a single Mi-24V, which was to serve as an object of study for the planned conversion of the Mi-24D to Mi-24V standard.

The political upheavals prevented these plans from being realized. On the advice of western politicians, the new East German government elected in March 1990 canceled all orders for weapons and instead paid high cancellation penalties to the Soviet manufacturers.

The existence of the NVA ended when East Germany joined the Federal Republic of Germany.

All of its attack helicopters were transferred to the *Bundeswehr* and were concentrated in Army Aviation Squadron East. The federal government gave one Mi-24D and one Mi-24P to the US, in part to make up for the Federal German refusal to take part in the first Gulf War against Iraq. Several Mi-24s underwent extensive testing by WTD-61 at Manching, while the rest flew occasionally to maintain airworthiness until 1993. There was no direct training or weapons training. When insufficient spares became available in 1993, many Mi-24s were given to Poland and Hungary; others ended up in museums. Today, ex-NVA Mi-24s are on display at the Gatow aviation museum and the Cottbus airfield museum, as well as in the military museum at Cottbus. The last flight by a German Mi-24 took place on September 14, 1994.

From the very beginning, the Mi-24 had no chance in the *Bundeswehr*. This was less due to its technical characteristics or any performance short-comings than to the *Bundeswehr*'s backward views on attack helicopters.

There had been attempts to arm the UH-1 helicopter in the Federal Republic of Germany in the 1960s, but these had been abandoned because it turned into a power struggle between the air force and army as to which should have the honor of supporting the ground troops from the air. The *Luftwaffe*'s argument that everything that flew over land belonged to it prevailed, and the army was left with just a few helicopters to defend against enemy armor in its own rear. The PAH-1 was developed from the BO105, a helicopter that was entirely capable of dealing with tanks but was scarcely suitable for any other purpose.

The military leadership was so opposed to the concept of the attack helicopter that even the use of the term "attack helicopter" was made taboo. Developments in this field, especially in the US but also in the east, were simply ignored.

Even when it became obvious that a successor to the PAH-1 was urgently needed, the PAH-2, from which the present-day Tiger would be developed,

Aircraft 521 was repaired after its crash and as 5211 was used as a training airframe at the military technical college in Bad Düben. *MTS Bad Düben*

was designed solely for use against tanks. It had neither effective armor protection nor an integral cannon and thus could not be used in an offensive role.

When the *Bundeswehr* took over an attack helicopter with a strongly offensive focus, conceptually it was simply overwhelmed. It had no idea what to do with the Mi-24, and so this outstanding weapons system was put on ice.

The *Bundeswehr* preferred to carry out foreign missions, such as the one in Somalia, with old carpet beaters such as the UH-1. These machines first had to be fitted with makeshift armor protection and then in the climatic conditions of Somalia were barely able to get into the air, to say nothing of being able to transport a reasonable load. The Mi-24, which was ideally suited to such a mission, was left at home because to Federal German politicians, attack helicopters had come to be seen as too martial. In the eyes of the politicians the *Bundeswehr* had become a sort of armed technical relief service; German soldiers were supposed to wave, drill wells, and set up schools for girls. If possible, they were to stay away from combat and therefore needed no support from attack helicopters.

By the time of Afghanistan at the latest, the reality looked very different.

During the ISAF mission, German troops had to watch as their Polish colleagues were protected by Mi-24s, some of which were ex-NVA machines, while they always had to ask for help from American helicopters. Detractors claimed that the politically motivated absence of the Mi-24 had cost the lives of German soldiers in Afghanistan.

Not until just before the end of the Afghanistan mission did German troops receive air support from their own Tiger attack helicopters. Operational experience showed that the mere appearance of an attack helicopter was sufficient to force the enemy onto the defensive and to protect the lives of soldiers on the ground. The Soviets had learned this lesson in Afghanistan three decades earlier.

Meanwhile the *Bundeswehr* has recognized the value of an attack helicopter. The term "attack helicopter" is no longer taboo, and there are again German attack helicopter wings. Sometimes the wheel has to be invented twice.

Mi-24 wearing the Iron Cross of the *Bundeswehr*. Unlike its service in the NVA, in Federal German service the Mi-24 also wore a nationality emblem under its fuselage. *Cottbus Airfield Museum*

Afterword

Mikhail Leontyevich Mil: The Father of the Mi-24

This final section is dedicated to the man who played the major role in the creation of the Mi-24: Mikhail Leontyevich Mil.

Mil was born in the Siberian city of Irkutsk on November 22, 1909. After completing school, at the age of seventeen he began studying at the technological institute in the city of Tomsk. Two years later he switched to the Don Polytechnic Institute, which was already specializing in aircraft design.

Mil completed his studies in 1931 and as a young engineer joined the TsAGI, the Central Aerodynamic Institute of the young Soviet Union, where he worked in a design bureau. In 1933, he took over the leadership of a collective engaged in aerodynamic calculations and experiments. It was there that he first came into contact with the problems of aerodynamic peculiarities of rotor-wing aircraft.

In addition to his theoretical work, Mil began working as a designer. He designed rotor blades and other aircraft components and looked into the characteristics of helicopters. Mil thus became involved in the design of the first Soviet helicopter.

In 1940, Mil was named deputy director of the new Factory No. 269. When Operation Barbarossa began on June 22, 1941, he was transferred to a reconnaissance squadron equipped with gyrocopters. This unit took part in the battle at Smolensk, which ultimately was lost by the Soviets.

In 1943, Mil returned to the TsAGI and resumed his research work in the field of rotor flight. He designed a first land-based helicopter, of which only a mockup was built.

In March 1947, Mil became the head of the newly created rotor flight laboratory within the TsAGI, which during 1947 developed into the OKB Mil design bureau.

Under his leadership, this design bureau produced the Mi-1 and Mi-4 helicopters in rapid succession. With the Mi-2 and Mi-8 he made the technological leap from piston to turboshaft engines. The Mi-6 became the first giant helicopter and was followed by the Mi-10 and its crane variant the Mi-10K, the Mi-14 naval helicopter, and ultimately the Mi-24 flying armored personnel carrier. Mil's largest helicopter, the Mi-12, flew as the V-12 prototype but did not enter production.

Mil initiated the founding of a scientific school for the training of helicopter designers. He and his successor trained thousands of students in specialty areas related to helicopters.

Mil was awarded high state decorations for his work. He became a hero of Soviet labor, won the Lenin Prize and the State Prize, and was awarded the Order of Lenin three times.

Mil died in 1970 at the age of sixty-one.

The helicopter designs developed by him proved to be outstanding and long lived; helicopters are still being built on the basis of the scheme developed by Mil. They have proved themselves in almost every country on earth and have demonstrated their outstanding reliability and performance under difficult conditions.

Mikhail
Leontyevich Mil,
1909–1970.
*Rostvertol PLC
Archive*

This Mi-24 monument is in front of the building occupied by the helicopter maker Rostvertol in Rostov on Don. *Samoilik via Rostvertol*

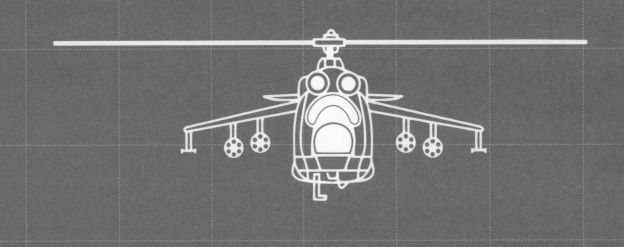
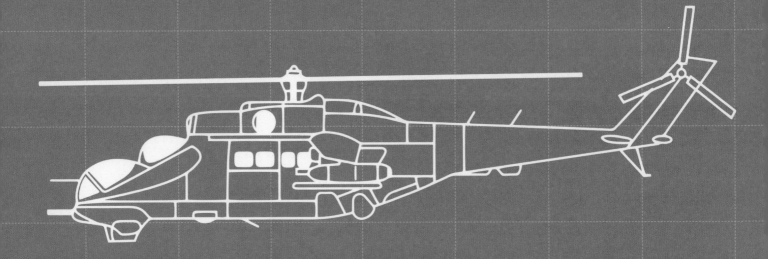